Malta and Gozo Buses

Tom Johnson
&
British Bus Publishing

Body codes used in the Bus Handbook series:

Type:

A	Articulated vehicle
B	Bus, either single-deck or double-deck
BC	Interurban - high-back seated bus
C	Coach
M	Minibus with design capacity of 16 seats or less
N	Low-floor bus (*Niederflur*), either single-deck or double-deck
O	Open-top bus (CO = convertible - PO = partial open-top)

Seating capacity is then shown. For double-decks the upper deck quantity is followed by the lower deck.

Door position:-

C	Centre entrance/exit
D	Dual doorway.
F	Front entrance/exit
R	Rear entrance/exit (no distinction between doored and open)
T	Three or more access points

Equipment:-

L	Lift for wheelchair	TV		Training vehicle.
M	Mail compartment	RV		Used as tow bus or engineer's vehicle.
T	Toilet	w		Vehicle is withdrawn and awaiting disposal.

e.g. - B32/28F is a double-deck bus with thirty-two seats upstairs, twenty-eight down and a front entrance/exit.
N43D is a low-floor bus with two or more doorways.

Regional books in the series:

The Scottish Bus Handbook
The Ireland & Islands Bus Handbook
The North East Bus Handbook
The Yorkshire Bus Handbook
The Lancashire, Cumbria and Manchester Bus Handbook
The Merseyside and Cheshire Bus Handbook
The East Midlands Bus Handbook
The West Midlands Bus Handbook
The Welsh Bus Handbook
The Eastern Bus Handbook
The South East Bus Handbook
The South West Bus Handbook

Annual books are produced for the major groups:

The Stagecoach Bus Handbook
The First Bus Handbook
The Arriva Bus Handbook
The London Bus Handbook
The National Express Handbook
Some editions for earlier years are available. Please contact the publisher.

Associated series:

The Hong Kong Bus Handbook
The Leyland Lynx Handbook
The Model Bus Handbook
The Postbus Handbook
The Overall Advertisment Bus Handbook - Volume 1
The Toy & Model Bus Handbook - Volume 1 - Early Diecasts
The Fire Brigade Handbook (fleet list of each local authority fire brigade)
The Fire Brigade Handbook - Special Appliances Volume 1
The Fire Brigade Handbook - Special Appliances Volume 2
The Police Range Rover Handbook

CONTENTS

Acknowledgments:

All photographs are by Tom Johnson unless otherwise shown. Readers wishing to learn about the complete history of buses on Malta are recommended to refer to "The Malta Bus" by Joseph Bonnici and Michael Cassar, first published in Malta in 1989.
The author is indebted to Emanuel and Maria Caruana and to Joe Scerri for all their help in drawing together the history of bus services on Gozo. Their reminiscences and anecdotes have added a personal flavour to this section of the book.

Nick Eyles and Garry Luck have collaborated with the author in the photographic section, as well as spending time travelling with him on Malta and Gozo. Thanks to them both.
Thanks too to Alan Edwards for his timely contribution, and to Paul Wigan and Michael Lee for their photographs, and David Donati for his help.
Pictured on the frontispiece, DBY 367 is one of the few modern low-floor buses imported during 1997. It is seen on a private duty at the tourist village near to the Golden Bay terminus on Easter Saturday evening 2001

This Edition - 2003 ISBN 1-897990-97-9

ISBN 1 897990 97 9

Published by *British Bus Publishing*
16 St Margaret's Drive, Telford, TF1 3PH
© Tom Johnson and British Bus Publishing, February 2003

INTRODUCTION

This book differs in approach from many others previously published by *British Bus Publishing*.

The number of vehicles on Malta and Gozo is small compared with the fleets of many British companies – no more than 1500 vehicles are listed in this book. However, the intention of the author has been to present a faithful and scenic profile of the buses and coaches in service on both islands in early 2003.

Each route bus on Malta and Gozo, and each coach is listed, accompanied by full technical details, current ownership and previous history. The islands' red minibuses are listed too, but generally only registrations are given, unless the vehicle is known NOT to be a Ford Transit.

Chapters about the bus routes on both Malta and Gozo, with route descriptions, details of sights to see and places to visit en route, timings and fares, also include a photograph of a vehicle in service somewhere along the route. Indeed, it has been the author's aim throughout to include photographs of vehicles in service around the island, rather than limiting views to Valletta's bus terminus around the Triton Fountain at the entrance to the capital city. Any bus enthusiast who has yet to visit Malta and Gozo will, it is hoped, be encouraged to pay a visit soon, if this series of photographs succeeds in its aim of presenting vehicles in service in picturesque, historical or architecturally interesting settings. Any tourist attracted to the buses by this book will find out about the bus he is travelling on and details about the island. The chapter on the history of Gozo routes is a personal reminiscence by two of the drivers on the island.

In writing this book, the author has received especial help from many people on Malta and Gozo. Victor Spiteri, Chairman of the ATP, Malta's Public Transport Association, has provided extensive up-to-date vehicle details and has generously replied to the author's frequent correspondence. Angelo Spiteri, Chairman of Garden of Eden Coaches, Leo Grech, Chairman of Paramount Coaches, the owners of Cancu Coaches and Zarb Coaches have all answered questions about their firms with humour and kindness. Joe Scerri, Emanuel Caruana, Joseph Apap and Antonio Xerri have provided the author with relevant contemporary details and historical data about Gozo vehicles. Paul Gatt, Executive Secretary at Naxxar Local Council, provided details about the town's unique bus services. Patrick Rausi at RMF Publishing provided the maps. The author expresses his grateful thanks to them all.

Finally, the author wishes to express his thanks to all the bus drivers whose vehicles feature in this book. Many of them have allowed him to take a photograph wherever and whenever he wished, whilst travelling on their vehicles. Their patience and forbearance are acknowledged here.

GEOGRAPHICAL SETTING

The Maltese archipelago lies some 96 kilometres south of Sicily in the Mediterranean Sea, equidistant from Gibraltar to the west and Alexandria to the east. There are three inhabited islands, Malta, Gozo and Comino, with three small uninhabited rocks, Cominetto, St Paul's Island and Filfla, which is now a bird sanctuary. About 350,000 people live on Malta in an area of 320 sq. km. There are about 26,000 residents on Gozo, which is about one third the size of Malta, and there are seven permanent residents on Comino.

One of the most recent rebuilds of a former British service bus to be seen on Malta in 2001 is FBY 787. Originally a Leyland Tiger Cub PSUC1/13 with East Lancs B45F bodywork with Blackburn Transport, it now carries a Scarnif Broadway body. In this photograph it awaits its next commitment on route 88 to Zebbug on 30th July 2001.

VEHICLES ON MALTA AND GOZO

In Malta, the capital, Valletta, is the main centre of bus operation. The majority of the routes on the island depart from the main bus terminus in Porta Reale which is overlooked by the Triton Fountain. The routes serve the main towns and villages throughout the island. In recent years some "Direct" services have been introduced, which provide faster and more convenient links between some of the principal holiday resorts and tourist areas, thus omitting Valletta altogether, and thereby obviating a change of bus en route.

There are 508 yellow route buses on Malta, which are allotted registration numbers from DBY 300 to 470, EBY 471 to 640 and FBY 641 to 807. All the buses are privately owned, and many are driven by their owners each day. The variety of buses in this fleet is Malta's attraction to the bus enthusiast. Normal control vehicles, now fifty years old, can still be seen in daily operation, along with slightly more modern vehicles with locally-built bodywork by firms such as Aquilina, Barbara, Brincat, Casha, Debono, Farrugia and Sammut. Some of these bodywork firms are even today (thirty years or more since they closed down) still well-represented; others far less so, with some, such as Farrugia, Xurrieq and Gauchi, being represented by just one or two vehicles carrying their bodywork. The chassis on which some of the older vehicles are built are no less interesting, with Thornycroft, Magirus Deutz, Indiana and Reo still represented in 2003. Enthusiasts from Great Britain will recognise many other vehicles which have been imported into Malta, after years of service in England and Wales, especially. Service buses from established British fleets, such as Crosville, Western National and Southern National, are represented by Bristol LH buses. Vehicles from municipal fleets, such as Blackburn, Hyndburn and Cynon Valley, as well as many Bedford and Ford coaches from independent companies all over GB are well represented. AEC Swifts from London Transport have been on the island for a minimum of fourteen years now, with the earliest being imported in 1980.

Whilst the transport enthusiast will find many interesting and some unique buses on the island, the age profile of the fleet causes concern in some quarters. New low-floor vehicles first appeared in Malta in 1997, when five 45-seater buses were delivered, an Optare Excel and four Dennis Darts. In July 2001 the first of the new regime of foreign vehicles arrived, a Chinese King Long low-floor bus. This vehicle marks the start of a planned renewal of the fleet over the next few years, with new low-floor buses - from Poland and China, for instance - likely to appear at regular intervals. The first low-floor bus built on the island, a Volvo chassis with locally-built Scarnif bodywork, is the precursor of others with Scarnif bodywork but on different chassis.

The provision and purchase of new vehicles for the Maltese owners has been a long and protracted affair. Back in 1995 almost 150 owners each paid a deposit of Lm500 towards the cost of their new bus. An agreement about the financing of the purchase of new buses was finally agreed just before Christmas 2001. These owners who paid the deposits will receive a government subsidy of Lm32,000 for each bus. The balance, which varies between Lm13,000 and Lm20,000 depending upon the make and model of the bus which the owner chooses, has to be paid by the owner.

The new buses have to comply with certain specifications laid down by the Authority. The low-floor buses will provide easy access for all, including senior citizens, the physically disabled and parents with prams. The maximum height from ground level to the first and only step must be no greater than 32cm. The vehicle's engine must be a turbo-charged diesel engine suitable for operation "in the local topographical, climatic and environmental conditions." Engine exhaust emissions have to meet the stringent Euro 1 conditions.

This book is published just as these wholesale changes are being introduced. Consequently the photographs show the fleet as in early 2003, with the old normal control buses still in service alongside a few low-floor vehicles. It therefore presents a picture of what has been the norm on the island for fifteen years or more, prior to the introduction of modern sophisticated buses which will, of necessity, force out many of the older vehicles.

The route buses operate on a "day on/day off" basis. A typical day's work lasts sixteen hours. The first timed departure on many of the routes is as early as 05:30 and buses operate on the same route throughout the day until as late as 22:00. The drivers are committed to operate according to a timetable provided by the PTA. This timetable is issued every fortnight and indicates which shift on which route each bus will operate each day during that two-week period.

On their days-off, drivers are allowed to use their buses on unscheduled work (for instance, in term-time, school journeys), to undertake private work or to carry out repairs. The number of bus departures throughout Malta on any day of the week averages about 4,700, with more during the peak summer months. Consequently on a summer's day, especially during June, July and August, the total number of vehicles in operation may exceed the average of 254 nominally in service. A network of night services has been widely advertised recently, too. The Sliema area is noted for its discotheques and evening entertainment and so there is a regular bus service from Sliema back to the principal villages on the island during the early hours each day.

The scheduled routes are designated merely by route numbers. Destinations are nowadays never displayed, although many of the buses of British origin retain their destination boards.

The route numbering system unites routes into areas; those routes passing through Marsa are numbered between 1 and 39; those passing through Msida from 40 to 69 with the Sliema routes numbered in the 60s, and those passing through Hamrun 70 to 94. All these routes depart from Valletta Porta Reale bus terminus. Route variations numbered above 100 reflect their partner route below 100. For instance route 38 and 138 serving Hagar Qim, or route 15 and 115 which serve Santa Lucia. The "Direct" routes on Malta link the principal holiday resorts and tourist centres, and in summer, especially, they provide a quick and frequent service for the holidaymakers on the island especially in Bugibba, Qawra and Sliema.

Fares are based on a zonal structure. Special tickets are also available for frequent travellers; 1-day, 3-day, 5-day and 7-day tickets entitle the holder to unlimited travel on the island's bus routes. Otherwise tickets are purchased from the driver of the bus, which in the height of summer can be a lengthy and time-consuming process on the popular tourist routes.

There are about 430 bus-owners on Malta who have their own collective organisation called the Public Transport Authority which was established by Act No. IX of 1989. Its remit is to "provide, regulate and promote an efficient, economical and secure public transport system on both land and sea". It has the task of overseeing the daily management of bus operation on the island, collecting the revenue, the profits of which are then shared out amongst the bus owners every fourteen days. In recent months it has committed itself to provide more information about the bus services on the island. In all bus termini in Malta, and in Victoria, Mgarr, Marsalforn and Xlendi on Gozo, notice boards have been erected displaying departure times of all services from that locality. At the Porte des Bombes and at Blata l-Bajda similar information is available about the all the routes serving those two locations. To relieve the problem of fare-collection highlighted above, the Authority is proceeding with the installation of bus ticketing machines on each bus. This automated scheme will, in so doing, provide the Authority with information about passenger usage on the buses, both on Malta and Gozo. Another aim of the Authority is to improve drivers' working conditions, by an alteration of the present daily commitments. It has been suggested that as many as 330 vehicles may be in operation each day, with two drivers allocated to each vehicle who would work on a shift-rota.

The Public Transport Authority is run by a committee of seven chosen from amongst the ranks of the 430 bus owners, and elected by the bus owners. The committee members serve for two years. The committee regularly meets the police and local councils to discuss mutual concerns. A board of discipline meets every fifteen days to oversee reports made by ticket inspectors and passengers. Contentious issues are formally discussed in the presence of an independent lawyer, so that as many as possible are resolved without court action.

In addition to the scheduled buses (the route buses) there is the Unscheduled Bus Service which runs a fleet of 155 coaches, about 400 minibuses, 200 taxis, and 82 horse-drawn cabs which are called *karozzini*. Many of the minibus owners belong to the Minibus Co-operative; some of the taxi-drivers are members of the White Taxi Service Amalgamated. Nowadays the 155 coaches boast a wide variety of livery styles and colours. Many of them are to be seen conveying holiday-makers to and from Malta International Airport at Luqa at the start and end of their holidays, or conveying them around the island on day-trips.

On Gozo there is now a fleet of 78 vehicles which comprises both service buses and more modern coaches. This is a twofold increase in the number of vehicles on the island from only about five years ago. It thus confirms the increase in popularity of Gozo as a tourist destination.

All the daily bus services depart from or near to the bus station in the island's capital, Victoria. In many cases an individual vehicle provides the service on each route day by day. However, the service to Mgarr Harbour which is the terminus for the ferry service to Malta demands more than one vehicle during the high tourist season. Coaches and buses all carry the same grey and red livery with a white roof, though the application of the red varies from bus to bus. Many of the newest coaches on Gozo are specially imported modern chassis with Malta-built bodies by Scarnif. Scarnif is an anagram of " Francis", the forename of the owner of the factory, Francis Attard. The coaches cater for the crowds of day-visitors to Gozo, many of whom are on excursions arranged by the tour operators at the hotels on Malta. Buses on Gozo, as in Malta, are owned by individual drivers, or, increasingly, by a firm which may have up to ten of the 78 buses on the island on its books. All seventy-eight vehicles are numbered sequentially from FBY 001 to FBY 079, without separate numbering schemes for route buses and coaches, as on Malta, with 069 omitted.

ROUTE BUSES ON MALTA

DBY 300	AEC Reliance 6MU2RA	Willowbrook	B46F	9/68	5/81	Charles Caruana, Mellieha
DBY 301	AEC Swift 4MP2RV	Marshall	B46F	1/71	11/00	Francis Galea, Fgura
DBY 302	*This registration is currently not in use.*					Carmel Abela, Zetjun
DBY 303	Bristol LH6L	Eastern Coach Works	B45F	11/76	7/87	Emanuele Camillieri, Mosta
DBY 304	Bristol LH6L	Eastern Coach Works	B45F	5/74	10/86	Charles Perrett, Gzira
DBY 305	AEC Swift 4MP2R	Park Royal	B46F	10/70	11/80	Evan Pace, Qormi
DBY 306	Leyland Royal Tiger PSU1/16	Aquilina (1973)	B45F	5/53	10/87	Stephen Cilia, Gharghur
DBY 307	Dennis Dart SLF	Plaxton Pointer	N45F	5/97	5/97	Leone Grech, Mosta
DBY 308	Maltese Docks/AEC f/c	Tonna	B40F	by 2/68	by 2/68	David Borg, Mellieha
DBY 309	Maltese Docks/Bedford	Barbara	B40F	4/67	4/67	Saviour Vella, Zejtun
DBY 310	Bedford YRQ	Duple Dominant I	C45F	1973	by10/88	John Abela, Zejtun
DBY 311	Ford 6	Aquilina	B36F	9/47	9/47	Joseph Psaila, Zurrieq
DBY 312	AEC Regal III 0962	Debono (1963)	B40F	1948	5/63	Raymond Buttigieg, Paola
DBY 313	Ford ET7	Casha	B36F	1953	by 2/68	Mario Pio Camilleri, Mosta
DBY 314	Bedford YLQ	Duple Dominant I	DP45F	5/76	by 1/85	Michael Micallef, Qormi
DBY 315	Leyland Comet	Sammut	B40F	by12/61	by 12/61	Stephen Cilia, Gharghur

DBY 300, Y-0300, Y-1001, A-0004, TNY 495G — Cynon Valley, 5
DBY 301, FBY 665, M-1530, EGN 200J. — Route bus, Malta (originally London Transport SMS200)
DBY 302
DBY 303, Y-0303, OCA 630P — Dragon Mechanical Services, Pembroke Dock (originally Crosville MS SLL630)
DBY 304, Y-0304, PTT 606M — Western National, 1606
DBY 305, Y-0305, Y-1006, A-0089, EGN 244J — London Transport, SMS 244 (originally B33D)
(*This vehicle was rebuilt in 1988, and again between 1994 and 1998*)
DBY 306, Y-0306, Y-0879, Y-1579, A-2908, 2908, MUF 650 — Unscheduled bus, Malta
DBY 307 — New
DBY 308, Y-0308, Y-1009, A-0117, 117 — New
DBY 309, Y-0309, Y-1010, A-0140, 140 — New
DBY 310, Y-0310, LBU 153L — Newton, Guildford
DBY 311, Y-0311, Y-1012, A-0146, 146 — New (*This vehicle was n/c until rebodied between '64 and '74*)
DBY 312, Y-0312, Y-1013, A-0158, 158, GNY 764 — Thomas, Port Talbot
DBY 313, Y-0313, Y-1014, A-0159, 159 — Of Maltese origin
DBY 314, Y-0314, LUX 543P — Cyril Evans, Senghenydd
DBY 315, Y-0315, Y-1016, A-0218, 218 — New

DBY 306 stands at the tree-lined square of Senglea, the terminus of route 3, on April 25th 2000.

DBY 326, newly repainted and recently back in public service in early 2002, is seen by the Trade School in Kalkara on route 4 at about midday on 24th March 2002.

DBY 316	Bedford YLQ	Duple Dominant II	C45F	1/78	by 3/86	Ronald Falzon, Marsa
DBY 317	Bedford SB	Barbara	B40F	1/62	1/62	George Xerri, Marsa
DBY 318	Maltese Docks/Bedford	Brincat/Cassar	B45F	unknown	by 4/73	Maria Rosaria Polidano, Kirkop
DBY 319	Bedford YRQ	Duple Dominant I	DP43F	5/73	by 1/84	John Desira, Bir-id-Deheb
DBY 320	Malta Docks/AEC	Debono	B36F	by12/68	by 10/90	Francis Caruana, Fgura
DBY 321	AEC Swift 4MP2R	Marshall	B53F	4/70	by 5/92	Mario Farrugia, Ghaxaq
DBY 322	Malta Docks/Bedford	Tonna	B39F	by 8/74	by 8/74	Rosaria Falzon, Fgura
DBY 323	Bedford YRQ	Duple Dominant I	C45F	4/73	by 4/85	Bartholomeo Muscat, Mgarr
DBY 324	Ford V8 f/c	Casha (1952)	B39F	by 1952	1952	Emmanuele Ellul, Bugibba
DBY 325	Bedford SBO	Grech/Schembri	B43F	by 12/52	by 2/52	Paul Axiaq, Bugibba
DBY 326	Bedford OB	Brincat	B36F	by 12/59	by 2/59	Joseph Borg, Zabbar
DBY 327	AEC CHMP3 f/c	Aquilina	DP36F	by 3/71	by 5/95	Victor Grech, Mosta
DBY 328	Bedford YLQ	Plaxton Panorama Elite III Exp	C45F	5/77	by 0/87	Vincent Camilleri, Mosta
DBY 329	Bedford OB f/c	Tonna (1974)	B40F	by 12/47	by 2/79	Joe Micallef, Qormi
DBY 330	Ford Cargo	Ramco (1999)	B45F	by 12/88	1/99	Alex Pulo, Paola

DBY 316, Y-0316, VNT 48S — Parry, Pwllheli

DBY 317, Y-0317, Y-1018, A-0234, 234 — New

DBY 318, Y-0318, Y-1019, A-0236, 236 — Of Maltese origin (*This vehicle was rebuilt by Cassar during 1998, and had re-entered service by April 1999*)

DBY 319, Y-0319, Y-1020, VBX 518L — Glyn Williams, Lower Tumble, 52

DBY 320, Y-0320, Y-0887, Y-1587, A -0699, 699 — Unscheduled coach, Malta

DBY 321, Y-0321, AML 13H — Ministry of Education, Malta (originally London Transport, SM 13)

DBY 322, Y-0322, Y-1023, A-0360, 360 — New

DBY 323, Y-0323, NLG 105L — Sheffield Health Authority

DBY 324, Y-0324, Y-1025, A-0454, 454 — Normal control vehicle

DBY 325, Y-0325, Y-1026, A-0529, 529 — New (*The 1980 body of this vehicle was rebuilt between 1998 and 2000*)

DBY 326, Y-0326, Y-0726, Y-1427, A-3291, 3291 — Route bus, Malta

DBY 327, Y-0327, Y-0850, Y-0868, Y-1568, A-7209, 7209 — Unscheduled bus, Malta

DBY 328, Y-0328, SUJ 974R — Glyn Evans, Manmoel

DBY 329, Y-0329, Y-1030, A-0557, A-2059, 2059 — Route bus, Malta

DBY 330 — Rebuild on lorry chassis

DBY 342 is seen at the terminus near Sliema ferries, between duties on route 652 to Golden Bay, on 10th April 2001.

DBY 331	AEC Reliance MU3RA	Debono (1969)	C45F	by 12/55	by 4/89	George Sammut, Mosta
DBY 332	Leyland Comet f/c	Schembri	B40F	by 12/50	1/54	Salvatore Vella, Zejtun
DBY 333	AEC Reliance ETS	Plaxton Supreme IV (1979)	DP47F	2/68	2/86	Emanuel Zarb, Mosta
DBY 334	Bedford YLQ	Plaxton Panorama Elite III	C45F	2/77	4/86	Charles Vella, Mosta
DBY 335	Bedford YRQ	Plaxton Panorama Elite II Exp	DP45F	1972	by 11/84	Emmanuel Mifsud, Qormi
DBY 336	Maltese Docks/ Bedford	Schembri	B40F	by 12/68	2/78	Paul Bezzina, Mosta
DBY 337	*This registration is currently not in use.*					Joe Abdilla, Safi
DBY 338	Albion CH51Y	Brincat (1976)	B45F	by 12/67	by 4/88	Joseph Falzon, Mosta
DBY 339	Bedford YLQ	Duple Dominant II	C45F	8/79	by 4/88	Etienne Falzon, Qormi
DBY 340	Leyland Tiger TS7	Barbara (1961)	B40F	1937	8/61	Charles Caruana, Mellieha
DBY 341	Maltese Docks f/c	Brincat	B40F	unknown	by 7/73	Emanuel Micallef, Mosta
DBY 342	Bedford SB8	Aquilina	B36F	6/62	6/00	Joseph Polidano, Kirkop
DBY 343	Bedford YRQ	Duple Dominant I	DP45F	8/74	5/85	Neville Sammut, San Gwann
DBY 344	Bedford YLQ	Duple Dominant IA	C45F	5/77	by 6/86	Z. S. Co. Ltd, Gzira

DBY 331, Y-0331, Y-0878, Y-1578, A-5573, 5573, HWH 450 — Unscheduled bus, Malta (formerly Dex, Rochdale)
DBY 332, Y-0332, Y-1033, A-0708, 708 — Rebuild on UK lorry chassis
DBY 333, KCY884, Y-0884, HPG650V, EJP561F — Unscheduled bus, Malta (formerly Thomas, West Ewell)(rebuilt from AEC Reliance 6MU3R in 1978, rebodied 1979)
DBY 334, Y-0344, RUT 390R — Camping, Brighton
DBY 335, Y-0335, XAW 326K — Williams, Brecon
DBY 336, Y-0336, Y-1037, A-0777, 777, 7054 — Private coach, Malta
DBY 337
DBY 338, Y-0338, Y-0854, Y-1554, A-7054, 7054 — Unscheduled bus, Malta
DBY 339, Y-0339, JWU 461V — Williams, Brecon
DBY 340, Y-0340, Y-1041, A-0856, 856, FW 8825 — Lincolnshire Road Car, 1446
DBY 341, Y-0341, Y-1042, A-0857, 857 — Maybe new vehicle
DBY 342, FBY 034, Y-0808, Y-1509, A-0143, 143 — Gozo bus
DBY 343, Y-0343, UJB 726N — Reliance, Newbury, 142
DBY 344, Y-0344, OAN 962R — Reliance, Newbury, 154

DBY 353 is seen at Qawra Bus Terminus on the evening of 11th April 2001 on lay-over between timings on route 49 to Valletta. The vehicle's attractive bodywork by Schembri is noteworthy for the roof-lights and distinctive radiator grill.

DBY 345	AEC Reliance 6MU2RA	Willowbrook	B45F	1968	5/81	Antonio Borg, Attard
DBY 346	AEC Regal III 0962	Zammit	B40F	1948	1962	Paul Buttigieg, Zabbar
DBY 347	Albion CD21 CXLW	Brincat	B45F	unknown	by 4/89	Francis Cortis, Naxxar
DBY 348	Dodge Kew	Daina	B45F	by 12/68	by 4/88	Alfred Xerri, Qormi
DBY 349	AEC Regal 0662	Barbara (1960)	B40F	1939	5/60	Michael Caruana, Birzebbugia
DBY 350	AEC Mercury	Farrugia	B40F	1960	5/65	Joseph Buhagiar, Zabbar
DBY 351	Bedford YRQ	Plaxton Panorama Elite II	DP45F	2/71	by 11/84	Nazzareno Caruana, Zabbar
DBY 352	Bristol LH6L	Eastern Coach Works	B45F	5/75	by 10/86	Gerald Sultana, Cospicua
DBY 353	Maltese Docks f/c	Schembri	B40F	1966	by 9/74	Victor Muscat, Naxxar
DBY 354	Bedford YLQ	Plaxton Panorama Elite III Exp	C45F	5/79	by 1/87	George Camilleri, Birkirkara
DBY 355	Ford R1014	Plaxton Panorama Elite III	C45F	2/78	by 4/85	Dennis Borg, Qrendi
DBY 356	Chevrolet f/c	Debono	B40F	by 12/56	by 12/56	Saviour Camilleri, Naxxar
DBY 357	Maltese Docks/AEC	Debono	B40F	9/62	9/62	Michael Spiteri, Qrendi
DBY 358	Bedford YLQ	Plaxton Panorama Elite III	C45F	4/77	by 4/85	Jeffrey Camilleri, Qormi
DBY 359	Bedford YLQ	Duple Dominant II	C45F	2/78	by 4/85	John Cassar, Kirkop
DBY 360	Bristol LH6L	Eastern Coach Works	B43F	12/73	by 11/95	Natasha Sammut, Gzira
DBY 361	Bedford QLD	Sammut	B40F	1944	6/68	Joseph Formosa, Birzebbugia
DBY 362	Bedford YRQ	Duple Dominant I	DP45F	12/74	by 10/86	Jonathan Mallia, Lija
DBY 363	Dodge f/c	Vella	B40F	unknown	by 7/73	George Cutajar, Tarxien
DBY 364	Bedford QL	Sammut	B36F	1943	by 9/74	Manuel Cutajar, Kirkup
DBY 365	Maltese Docks f/c	Schembri	B40F	unknown	by 6/74	Horace Vella, Qormi
DBY 366	Bedford YRQ	Duple Dominant I	DP45F	1973	by 11/84	Anton Gatt, Zetjun
DBY 367	Dennis Dart SLF	East Lancs Spryte	N45F	3/97	3/97	Leone Grech, Mosta
DBY 368	Reo Speedwagon	Aquilina	B36F	by 12/37	by 12/55	Mario Farrugia, Attard
DBY 369	AEC Reliance 2MU3RA	Spiteri (1974)	B45F	1961	by 3/87	Peter Pace, Qrendi
DBY 370	Bedford SB	Barbara	B40F	5/69	11/75	Paul Mifsud, Mellieha
DBY 371	Bedford SB8	Debono	B40F	4/62	4/62	Antonio Xerri, Fgura
DBY 372	Ford ET7 f/c	Casha (1974)	B40F	unknown	by 4/64	Joseph Zammit, Qormi
DBY 373	Bedford YRQ	Scarnif (1994)	B45F	9/74	by 10/86	Nazzareno Abela, Zetjun
DBY 374	AEC Mercury 2GM4RH	Barbara	B40F	unknown	3/68	Grezzju Borg, Zabbar
DBY 375	Bedford SBG	Aquilina (1966)	B45F	by 12/55	4/66	Carmelo Borg, Rabat

DBY 375 pauses at the road junction at the end of Triq il-Knisja in Xghajra before turning right along the coast road at the northern end of its run from Valletta on 29th July 2001.

DBY 345, Y-0345, Y-1046, A-0915, TNY 494G	Cynon Valley, 4
DBY 346, Y-0346, Y-1047, A-0921, 921, HYP 309	Catt & Swann, Great Bromley
DBY 347, Y-0347, Y-0891, Y-1591	Unscheduled bus, Malta
DBY 348, Y-0348, Y-0886, Y-1586, A-2128, 2128	Unscheduled bus, Malta
DBY 349, Y-0349, Y-1050, A-0983, 983, HFC 413	City of Oxford, 6
DBY 350, Y-0350, Y-1051, A-0897, 897	Of unknown origin
DBY 351, Y-0351, XVY 198J	Tozer, Scarborough, 4
DBY 352, Y-0352, HBX 948N	Davies Bros., Pencader, 97
DBY 353, Y-0353, Y-1054, A-1058, 1058	Of unknown origin
DBY 354, Y-0354, TEJ 102T	Evans, Penrhyncoch
DBY 355, Y-0355, XEF 936S, 3996 EL, XHS 122S	Drew, Guisborough
DBY 356, Y-0356, Y-1057, A-1116, 1116	New
DBY 357, Y-0357, Y-1058, A-1121, 1121	New
DBY 358, Y-0358, UWU 628R	Collin, East Hardwick
DBY 359, Y-0359, BTU 655S	Bostock, Congleton, 10
DBY 360, Y-0360, Y-0705, NFJ 596M	Route bus, Malta: (originally Western National, 1576)
DBY 361, Y-0361, Y-1062, A-1181, 1181	Of unknown origin
DBY 362, Y-0362, STM 725N	Ouse Valley, Goldington
DBY 363, Y-0363, Y-1064, A-1212, 1212	Normal control bus, Malta
	(*This vehicle was re-panelled by Vella during 1997/98*)
DBY 364, Y-0364, Y-1065, A-1242, 1242, 699	Route bus, Malta
DBY 365, Y-0365, Y-1066, A-1290, 1290	Route bus, Malta
DBY 366, Y-0366, BUX 235L	Glyn Williams, Lower Tumble, 4
DBY 367	New (*This vehicle has a manual gearbox*)
DBY 368, Y-0368, Y-1069, A-1306, 1306, 2370	Route bus, Malta
DBY 369, Y-0369, Y-0903, Y-1603, A-0434, 434, RDB 860	Unscheduled bus, Malta: (originally North Western, 890)
DBY 370, Y-0370, Y-1071, A-1346, 1346, 5571	Route bus, Malta
DBY 371, Y-0371, Y-1072, A-1390, 1390	New
DBY 372, Y-0372, Y-1073, A-1403, 1403	n/c route bus , Malta
DBY 373, Y-0373, SYO 601N	Wilder, Byfleet (*This vehicle carries the sign*
	"The Maltese Bus" and was the first bus rebuilt by Scarnif)
DBY 374, Y-0374, Y-1075, A-1418, 1418	Of Maltese origin
DBY 375, Y-0375, Y-1076, A-1421, 1421, 33 RN 78	Ministry of Defence

DBY 382, the venerable Thornycroft, is seen at Valletta Bus Terminus in between journeys on the circular route 41 to San Gwann, on 8th August 2001. Its side advertisement encourages the use of public transport for a cleaner environment.

DBY 376	Bedford SB	Mifsud	B40F	unknown	by 10/88	Leone Grech, Mosta
DBY 377	Magirus Deutz f/c	Sammut	B40F	unknown	by 3/73	Joseph Buttigieg, Zabbar
DBY 378	Leyland Tiger Cub PSUC1/13	East Lancs	B46F	1966	5/81	Horace Vella, Qormi
DBY 379	AEC Swift 4MP2R	Marshall	B46F	4/70	by 5/81	Saviour Grech, Mqabba
DBY 380	AEC Swift 4MP2R1	Park Royal	B46F	9/70	by 5/81	Anthony Debono, Mqabba
DBY 381	Maltese Docks/Bedford	Brincat	B39F	7/67	7/67	Charles Calleja, Naxxar
DBY 382	Thornycroft Sturdy	Brincat	B35F	1948	1948	John Borg, Mellieha
DBY 383	Bedford YRQ	Plaxton Panorama Elite II	DP45F	10/71	by 4/85	Wistin Muscat, San Pawl Il-Bahar
DBY 384	Maltese Docks/Bedford	Barbara	B40F	11/68	11/68	Charlie Borg, Mellieha
DBY 385	Bedford YLQ	Plaxton Panorama Elite III Exp	C45F	4/77	by 1/87	Charlie Abela, Zejtun
DBY 386	Bedford SB	Sladden	C40F	unknown	by 4/94	Angelo Abela, Rabat
DBY 387	Maltese Docks f/c	Barbara	B36F	3/72	3/72	Alex Sammut, Birkirkara
DBY 388	Bedford QL	Casha	B40F	unknown	by 3/75	Mario Jasmine Farrugia, Tarxien
DBY 389	AEC Swift 4MP2R1	Park Royal	B47F	1/71	9/81	Alexander Borg, Zebbug
DBY 390	Bedford f/c	Brincat	B40F	by 4/64	by 4/64	Carmel Abela, Zejtun

DBY 376, Y-0376, Y-0869, Y-1569, A-0232, 232   Unscheduled bus, Malta
DBY 377, Y-0377, Y-1078, A-1517, 1517   Of Maltese origin
DBY 378, Y-0378, Y-1079, A-1526, YTD 290D   Blackburn, 10
DBY 379, Y-0379, Y-1080, A-1557, AML 20H   London Transport, SM20
DBY 380, Y-0380, Y-1081, A-1585, EGN 232J   London Transport, SMS 232 (*This vehicle underwent refurbishment during late 2000 and early 2001, and re-entered service in April 2001.*)

DBY 381, Y-0381, Y-1082, A-1604, 1604   New
DBY 382, Y-0382, Y-1083, A-1606, 1606   New
DBY 383, Y-0383, Y-1084, AJH 128K   Bantam, Ipswich
DBY 384, Y-0384, Y-1085, A-1643, 1643   New
DBY 385, Y-0385, RBO 669R   Williams, Brecon
DBY 386, Y-0386, Y-0853, Y-1553, A-2681, 2681   Unscheduled bus, Malta
DBY 387, Y-0387, Y-1088, A-1721, 1721   New
DBY 388, Y-0388, Y-1089, A-1723, 1723   Of Maltese origin
DBY 389, Y-0389, Y-1090, A-1751, EGN 329J   London Transport, SMS 329
DBY 390, Y-0390, Y-1091, A-1754, 1754   New

DBY 397 heads towards the outskirts of Qrendi after serving the Blue Grotto and Hagar Qim temples on route 38 on Easter Monday afternoon 2001.

DBY 391	Bedford f/c	Debono	B36F	by 9/74	by 12/84	Pacifico Cutajar, Zebbug
DBY 392	Bedford SB	Aquilina	B40F	unknown	by 6/68	Donald Vince Borg, Mellieha
DBY 393	Bedford SBG	Casha	B40F	1955	by 12/92	Paul Cutajar, Siggiewi
DBY 394	Mercedes Benz 312	Casha	B40F	1960	by 5/91	Carmelo Farrugia, Zejtun
DBY 395	Bedford f/c	Casha	B46F	8/62	by 3/73	George Galea, Sliema
DBY 396	Bedford f/c	Debono	B36F	by 12/58	by 12/58	Salvu Sciberras, Zabbar
DBY 397	GMC f/c	Tonna	B40F	unknown	by 8/74	Siliano Sammut, Mosta
DBY 398	Maltese Docks/Bedford f/c	Brincat	B40F	3/63	3/63	Francis Galea, Fgura
DBY 399	Ford ET7	Casha	B40F	by 12/57	by 12/69	Joseph Mallia, Lija
DBY 400	Bedford YRQ	Plaxton Panorama Elite III E	C45F	3/73	by 9/85	Pasquale Sciberras, Mqabba
DBY 401	Leyland TS4	Debono (1952)	B40F	1932	5/52	Francis Galea, Fgura
DBY 402	Leyland Royal Tiger PSU1/16	Aquilina	B45F	1951	by 10/91	Carmelo Caruana, Zebbug
DBY 403	Bedford SBG	Tonna	B40F	1955	by 8/74	John Zammit, Qormi
DBY 404	Bedford SBO	Sammut	B40F	1954	by 11/95	John Borg, Zejtun
DBY 405	Ford R192	Plaxton Panorama Elite III	C45F	3/74	by 9/85	Francis Galea, Fgura
DBY 406	Bedford YRQ	Plaxton Panorama Elite II Exp	C45F	5/75	by 6/89	Natasha Zammit, Gzira
DBY 407	Ford V8 f/c	Brincat	B39F	by 12/59	by 12/59	Tarcisio Gatt, Marsaskala

DBY 391, Y-0391, Y-1092, A-1258, 1258   Route bus, Malta
DBY 392, Y-0392, Y-1093, A-1764, 1764   Of Maltese origin
DBY 393, Y-0393, Y-1094, A-1767, 1767   Ministry of Supply
DBY 394, Y-0394, Y-0913, Y-1613, A-4755, 4755   Unscheduled bus, Malta
DBY 395, Y-0395, Y-1096, A-1784, 1784   Of Maltese origin
DBY 396, Y-0396, Y-1097, A-1793, 1793   New
DBY 397, Y-0397, Y-1098, A-1795, 1795   Of Maltese origin
DBY 398, Y-0398, Y-1099, A-1803, 1803   New
DBY 399, Y-0399, Y-1100, A-1804, 1804   Of Maltese origin
DBY 400, Y-0400, CPY 580L   Carnell, Sutton Bridge
DBY 401, Y-0401, Y-1102, A-1823, 1823   Unknown UK operator
DBY 402, Y-0402, Y-0885, Y-1585, A-2846, 2846   Unscheduled bus, Malta
DBY 403, Y-0403, Y-1104, A-1832, 1832   Ministry of Supply
DBY 404, Y-0404, Y-0557, Y-0595, Y-1296, A-2765, 2765   Route bus, Malta
DBY 405, Y-0405, VYC 869M   Andrews, Marshfield
DBY 406, Y-0406, KUR 304P   Fletcher, Skelmersdale
DBY 407, Y-0407, Y-1108, A-1859, 1859   New

DBY 425, the unique Magirus Deutz route bus, is parked at Cirkewwa Ferry on Easter Sunday afternoon, 2001.

DBY 408	Bedford SB	Mulliner/Vella	B36F	by 8/74	by 8/74	Joseph Refalo, Hamrun
DBY 409	Bedford SB1	Debono	B40F	by12/59	by 12/59	Raymong Borg, Mellieha
DBY 410	Bedford YLQ	Duple Dominant II	C45F	4/78	by 4/89	Joseph Farrugia, San Gwann
DBY 411	Bedford YRQ	Duple Dominant I	C45F	4/74	by 4/85	Emanuele Galea, Gzira
DBY 412	Bedford YRQ	Duple Dominant I	C45F	5/74	by 1/87	Geirge Buhagiar, Marsa
DBY 413	Mercedes Benz 312	Casha	B40F	by 12/60	by 10/88	Carmel Borg, Mellieha
DBY 414	Bedford YLQ	Duple Dominant I	C45F	3/77	11/84	Michael Micallef, Qormi
DBY 415	Dodge f/c	Aquilina	B40F	by 2/68	1979	Stephen Zammit, Siggiewi
DBY 416	Dodge f/c	Vella	B36F	by 12/52	by 4/89	Filippa d'Amato, Zebbug
DBY 417	Bedford YRQ	Plaxton Panorama Elite III	C45F	4/75	9/84	Gaetano Sciberras, Kirkop
DBY 418	Bedford YLQ	Plaxton Panorama Elite III	C45F	1/77	by 9/85	Josephine Sammut, San Gwann
DBY 419	Leyland Hippo	Scarnif (1995)	B45F	by 12/40	4/94	John Mary Cachia, Gudja
DBY 420	AEC Swift 4MP2R1	Park Royal	B46F	4/71	by 8/81	Silvio Buttigieg, Zetjun
DBY 421	Magirus Deutz O3500	Debono	B36F	1956	1956	Gerald Camilleri, Naxxar
DBY 422	Bristol LH6L	Eastern Coach Works	B45F	2/74	by 3/86	Josephine Cortis, Naxxar

DBY 408, Y-0408, Y-1109, A-1860, 1860 — Royal Navy (*This vehicle has a Vella reconstruction of the original Mulliner body, which was carried out in 1974*)

DBY 409, Y-0409, Y-1110, A-1861, 1861 — New

DBY 410, Y-0410, TPJ 274S — Ron's, Ashington

DBY 411, Y-0411, Y-1112, XTH 700M — Ffoshelig Motors, Newchurch

DBY 412, Y-0412, VNK 480M — Reid, Bedford

DBY 413, Y-0413, Y-0912, Y-1612, A-0441, 441 — Unscheduled bus, Malta

DBY 414, Y-0414, Y-1115, STT 962R — Cyril Evans, Senghenydd

DBY 415, Y-0415, Y-1116, A-1900, A-3209, 3209 — Route bus, Malta

DBY 416, Y-0416, Y-0874, Y-1574, A-7206, 7206 — Unscheduled bus, Malta

DBY 417, Y-0417, Y-1118, KCK 539N — Parfitt's, Rhymney Bridge

DBY 418, Y-0418, RRR 905R — Mowbray, Stanley

DBY 419, Y-0419, Y-0321, Y-0646, Y-1347, A-2981, 2981 — Route bus, Malta

DBY 420, Y-0420, Y-1121, A-1952, EGN 427J — Leybourne Grange Hospital, West Malling (originally London Transport, SMS 427)

DBY 421, Y-0421, Y-1122, A-1956, 1956 — New

DBY 422, Y-0422, NLJ 523M — Hants and Dorset, 3523

EBY 433 is one of the latest low-floor route bus to enter service. It is seen on the afternoon of 2nd December 2002 arriving at Valletta Porta Reale bus terminus, on what is believed to be its first day in service. *Alan*

Reg	Type	Body	Seating			Owner
DBY 423	Maple Leaf f/c	Schembri	B40F	by 12/48	by 4/64	Joseph Zammit, San Gwann
DBY 424	Bedford YRQ	Duple Dominant Express I	C45F	6/74	by 9/85	Joseph Refalo, Hamrun
DBY 425	Bedford YLQ	Duple Dominant II	DP45F	2/78	by 4/85	Alexander Bonavia, Naxxar
DBY 426	AEC Swift 4MP2R	Marshall	B46F	6/70	by 8/81	Rosaria Falzon, Zabbar
DBY 427	Leyland Leopard PSU4B/2R	Marshall	B46F	11/72	10/90	Francis Galea, Fgura
DBY 428	Dodge f/c	Casha	B40F	1956	by 4/90	Carmelo Abela, Rabat
DBY 429	Unknown f/c	Barbara	B40F	1938	7/59	Patrick Cauchi, Mellieha
DBY 430	Dodge f/c	Schembri	B36F	unknown	by 9/69	Maria Buttigieg, Marsaskala
DBY 431	Bedford YLQ	Duple Dominant Bus	B46F	3/75	by 6/91	Saviour Abela, Birzebbugia
DBY 432	*This registration is currently not in use.*					Victor Galea, Mosta
EBY 433	Solaris Urbino	Solaris	N45F	11/02	11/02	Mario Mifsud, Mgarrr
DBY 434	Indiana f/c	Aquilina	B40F	by 12/38	by 8/54	Joseph Cassar, Rabat
DBY 435	Maltese Docks/AEC	Barbara	B36F	2/66	2/66	John Abela, Zetjun
DBY 436	Bedford SB	Casha	B40F	1952	by 8/74	Carmelo Mangion, Marsa
DBY 437	Ford R1014	Plaxton Panorama Elite III	C45F	8/78	by 1/87	John Desira, Zabbar

DBY 423, Y-0423, Y-1124, A-1959, 1959   Route bus, Malta (*This vehicle was rebuilt to f/c from n/c in 1964 and rebodied by Schembri at that time.*)

DBY 424, Y-0424, SNX 601M   Tanat Valley, Pentrefelin
DBY 425, Y-0425, BTU 654S   Bostock, Congleton, 33
DBY 426, Y-0426, Y-1127, A-1971, AML 15H   London Transport, SM 15
DBY 427, Y-0427, GKE 457L   Wealden, Five Oak Green
DBY 428, Y-0428, Y-1181, A-2237, 2237   Route bus, Malta
DBY 429, Y-0429, Y-1130, A-1977, 1977   Unknown UK operator
(*This vehicle is believed to have an SOS chassis, ex-BMMO Midland Red*)

DBY 430, Y-0430, Y-1131, A-1979, 1979   Of unknown origin
DBY 431, Y-0431, NKE 303P   Penjon, Benenden
DBY 432
EBY 433   New (*Note that this vehicle was allocated an out-of-sequence EBY registration*)

DBY 434, Y-0434, Y-1135, A-2002, 2002   n/c route bus, Malta
DBY 435, Y-0435, Y-1136, A-2003, 2003   New
DBY 436, Y-0436, Y-1137, A-2007, 2007   Ministry of Supply
DBY 437, Y-0437, SUO 247T   Evans, Tregaron

DBY 460 is seen at Valletta Bus Terminus on July 28th, 2001. Notice its distinctive frontal treatment, especially its large and clear route number indicator.

DBY 438	Maltese Docks/AEC MP	Farrugia	B40F	8/66	8/66	Anthony Falzon, Qormi
DBY 439	Maltese Docks/Bedford	Aquilina	B40F	10/62	10/62	Carmel Vella, Birzebbugia
DBY 440	*This registration is currently not in use.*					Joe Abela, Ghaxaq
DBY 441	Bedford YRQ	Plaxton Panorama Elite III	DP45F	6/74	by 1/85	John Abela, Zetjun
DBY 442	Bedford YLQ	Plaxton Panorama Elite III	C45F	1/77	by 8/86	John Xerri, Mosta
DBY 443	Dodge f/c	Aquilina	B40F	by 9/54	by 3/69	Alex Farrugia, Mgarr
DBY 444	Leyland Royal Tiger PSU1/13	East Lancs/Scarnif	B45F	1967	by 6/82	Joseph Buhagiar, Zebbug
DBY 445	Albion VT17ALHD	Barbara	B36F	9/67	9/67	Michael Pace, Naxxar
DBY 446	Ford V8 f/c	Barbara	B40F	6/50	6/50	Kristinu Giordmaina, Siggiewi
DBY 447	Bedford YRQ	Duple Dominant I	C45F	8/75	by 8/86	John Mary Sacco, Qrendi
DBY 448	Ford V8 f/c	Zammit (1961)	B40F	3/38	3/38	Raymond Buttigieg, Zabbar
DBY 449	Bedford YRQ	Duple Dominant Express I	C45F	9/75	3/86	Eugenio Zammit, Qormi
DBY 450	AEC Mercury	Aquilina	B40F	1956	by 10/88	Antoine Sant, Mellieha
DBY 451	Bedford SBG	Tonna	B40F	1954	by 8/74	Bartolomeo Sammut, San Gwann
DBY 452	Bedford SB	Aquilina	B40F	10/58	10/58	Paul Cutajar, Luqa
DBY 453	Bedford YRQ	Plaxton Panorama Elite III	DP45F	1/73	by 10/86	Natasha Sammut, Gzira
DBY 454	Ford ET7	Aquilina	B36F	3/52	3/52	Victor Mifsud, Mgarr
DBY 455	Bedford f/c	Debono	B36F	by 5/72	by 3/87	Rosaria Falzon, Fgura
DBY 456	Bedford f/c	Aquilina	B40F	8/63	8/63	Carmel Cassar, Kalkara
DBY 457	Bedford YLQ	Plaxton Panorama Elite III	C45F	1/77	by 8/86	Nicholas Grech, Mqabba
DBY 458	Leyland Royal Tiger PSU1/15	Aquilina (1972)	B44F	1951	by 4/88	Francis Galea, Fgura
DBY 459	Ford R1014	Plaxton Panorama Elite III	C45F	4/80	by 4/89	Emmanuele d'Amato, Siggiewi
DBY 460	Bedford SB	Brincat	B41F	by 4/55	by 12/91	Nicholas Grech, Mqabba
DBY 461	Maltese Docks f/c	Schembri	B40F	unknown	by 6/89	Gerald Sultana, Cospicua
DBY 462	Dennis Dart SLF 10.6m	Plaxton Pointer	N45F	5/97	5/97	Leone Grech, Mosta
DBY 463	Bedford SBO	Barbara	B46F	1955	by 6/89	Horace Vella, Qormi
DBY 464	Dodge f/c	Zammit	B40F	unknown	by 8/74	Raymond Buttigieg, Zabbar
DBY 465	Bedford SB	Borg (1966)	B41F	unknown	1966	Carmel Grech, Zabbar
DBY 466	AEC Swift 4MP2R	Marshall	B53F	4/70	by 5/91	Joseph Abela, Ghaxaq
DBY 467	Bedford YRQ	Marshall	B46F	7/75	by 3/90	Mario Abela, Zejtun
DBY 468	Bedford SB	Brincat (1972)	B40F	unknown	by 4/88	George Buhagiar, Marsa
DBY 469	Bristol LH6L	Eastern Coach Works	B45F	12/74	by 9/85	Albert Sammut, San Gwann
DBY 470	Bristol LH6L	Eastern Coach Works	B45F	12/74	by 8/86	Marco Borg, San Gwann

DBY 454 sets off from Balluta Bay on route 68 to Bahar ic-Caghaq on 29th March 2002.

DBY 438, Y-0438, Y-1139, A-2018, 2018	New
DBY 439, Y-0439, Y-1140, A-2022, 2022	New
DBY 440	
DBY 441, Y-0441, Y-1142, SHE 199M	Morley, West Row
DBY 442, Y-0442, RGS 98R	McAndrew, Leamington Spa
DBY 443, Y-0443, Y-1144, A-2064, 2064, 3280	Route bus, Malta
DBY 444, Y-0444, Y-1145, GBV 17E	Blackburn, 17 (*This vehicle was rebuilt during 2000*)
DBY 445, Y-0445, Y-1146, A-2083, 2083	New
DBY 446, Y-0446, Y-1147, A-2084, 2084	New
DBY 447, Y-0447, JVJ 442P	Camping, Brighton
DBY 448, Y-0448, Y-1149, A-2091, 2091	New
DBY 449, Y-0449, JWO 48P	Bebb, Llantwit Fardre
DBY 450, Y-0450, Y-0894, Y-1594, A-2625, 2625	Unscheduled bus, Malta
DBY 451, Y-0451, Y-1152, A-2103, 2103	Ministry of Supply
DBY 452, Y-0452, Y-1153, A-2109, 2109	New
DBY 453, Y-0453, FNL 581L	Waldron and Grange, Nottingham (*This vehicle was refurbished during late 2000 and summer 2001*)
DBY 454, Y-0454, Y-1155, A-2114, 2114	New
DBY 455, Y-0455, Y-0890, Y-1590, A-0634, 634	Unscheduled bus, Malta
DBY 456, Y-0456, Y-1157, A-2121, 2121	New
DBY 457, Y-0457, SHE 938R	Ganal, Shotts
DBY 458, Y-0458, Y-0898, Y-1598, A-3326, 3326, DRN 703	Unscheduled bus, Malta
DBY 459, Y-0459, GYJ 955V	Dunn-Line, Nottingham
DBY 460, Y-0460, Y-0910, Y-1610, A-4873, 4873	Unscheduled bus, Malta
DBY 461, Y-0461, Y-0604, Y-1162, A-2819, 2819	Route bus, Malta
DBY 462	New
DBY 463, Y-0463, Y-0459, Y-1160, A-2135,2135	Route bus, Malta
DBY 464, Y-0464, Y-1165, A-2162, 2162	Of unknown origin
DBY 465, Y-0465, Y-1166, A-2164, 2164	Royal Navy
DBY 466, Y-0466, M-1589, AML 18H	Ministry of Education, Malta (originally London Transport, SM 18)
DBY 467, Y-0467, HGM 613N	Atomic Weapons Research Establishment, Aldermaston
DBY 468, Y-0468, Y-0908, Y-1608, A-2139, 2139	Unscheduled bus, Malta
DBY 469, Y-0469, GDV 464N	Southern National, 107
DBY 470, Y-0470, GDV 458N	Western National, 1609

DBY 482 bides its time at Mellieha (Ghadira Bay), the terminus of route 44, after returning from Popeye Village (on route 441) on 26th August 2000. The distinctive destination board used for the Popeye Village route is clearly visible, placed over the route indicator box in the windscreen.

EBY 471	Leyland f/c	Aquilina (1969)	B45F	unknown	2/69	Alfred Cassar, Zabbar
EBY 472	unknown f/c	Casha	B40F	unknown	by 10/87	Alfred Mercieca, Marsa
EBY 473	Ford R1014	Caruana	B45F	1978	by 6/92	Alex Sammut, Birkirkara
EBY 474	Bedford YRQ	Duple Dominant I	C45F	1/75	by 11/84	Mario Buhagiar, Zabbar
EBY 475	Bedford YRQ	Plaxton Panorama Elite III	C45F	4/76	by 1/87	Saviour Zahra, Rabat
EBY 476	Bristol LH6L	Eastern Coach Works	B45F	1/75	by 3/90	Carmel Abela, Zejtun
EBY 477	Bedford YLQ	Plaxton Panorama Elite III	C45F	8/78	by 1/87	Carmel Xerri, Qormi
EBY 478	Ford ET7 f/c	Brincat	B41F	1954	4/90	Carlos Cardona, Mosta
EBY 479	Leyland Leopard PSU4/4R	Marshall	B45F	4/68	by 5/81	Michael Cutajar, Kirkop
EBY 480	Bedford YLQ	Duple Dominant I	C45F	8/76	by 10/87	Carmel Borg, Rabat
EBY 481	*This registration is currently not in use.*					Grezzju Borg, Zabbar
EBY 482	Dodge f/c	Aquilina (1955)	B40F	unknown	12/55	Noel Vella, Mellieha
EBY 483	Maltese Docks f/c	Barbara	B40F	by 12/62	2/78	Mario Cassar, Mosta
EBY 484	Leyland f/c	Barbara	B40F	unknown	by 3/87	Raymond Buttigieg, Zabbar
EBY 485	Bedford YLQ	Plaxton Panorama Elite III	C45F	4/78	by 10/87	Horace Vella, Qormi
EBY 486	Bedford f/c	Aquilina	B36F	1971	by 2/91	Reuben Galea, Msida
EBY 487	Bedford f/c	Aquilina	B40F	unknown	1/56	Jimmy Bonavia, Zabbar

EBY 471, Y-0471, Y-1172, A-2217, 2217 — Route bus, Malta
EBY 472, Y-0472, Y-1173, A-2218, 2218 — Rebuilt route bus, Malta
EBY 473, XBH 859S — Town and Around, Folkestone, (*This vehicle was extensively rebuilt by March 2002*)
EBY 474, Y-0474, GUX 402N — Squirrel, Hitcham
EBY 475, Y-0475, A111 MAN, SBV 284P — Tours Isle of Man, Douglas, 20
EBY 476, Y-0476, GLJ 487N — I. M. Museum, Southsea (originally Hants and Dorset, 3555)
EBY 477, Y-0477, YRY 509T — Evans, Tregaron
EBY 478, Y-0478, Y-0501, Y-0921, Y-1621, A-2255, 2255 — Route bus, Malta
EBY 479, Y-0479, Y-1180, A-2236, NHE 10F — West Yorkshire PTE, 3360
EBY 480, Y-0480, Y-1181, OWV439R — Plumpton Coaches
EBY 481
EBY 482, Y-0482, Y-1183, A-2247, 2247 — Of Maltese origin
EBY 483, Y-0483, Y-1184, A-2253, 2253, 3117 — Route bus, Malta
EBY 484, Y-0484, Y-0865, Y-1565, A-7244, 7244 — Unscheduled bus, Malta
EBY 485, Y-0485, ANR 741T — Cropper, Leeds
EBY 486, Y-0486, Y-0858, Y-1558, A-0192, 192 — Unscheduled bus, Malta
EBY 487, Y-0487, Y-1188, A-2269, 2269 — Of Maltese origin

EBY 499 seen close to Valletta Porta Reale bus terminus on 28th July 2001. This bus is a true island dweller having spent its early life on the Isle of Wight.

EBY 488	MAN 14.220 HOCL-NR	Scarnif	N?F	12/02	12/02	Paul Buhagiar, Dingli
EBY 489	*This registration is currently not in use.*					Gerald Sultana, San Gwann
EBY 490	Ford R1014	Plaxton Panorama Elite III	C45F	1/79	by 7/88	Joseph Abela, Birzebbugia
EBY 491	Bedford YRQ	Plaxton Elite Express III	DP45F	7/75	by 4/85	Luke Borg, Qormi
EBY 492	Albion CH	Aquilina (1975)	B41F	unknown	by 8/86	Carmel Dalli, Gzira
EBY 493	Bedford YRQ	Duple Dominant I	C45F	8/74	by 4/85	Francis Galea, Fgura
EBY 494	Bedford RL	Zammit	B40F	1945	by 8/74	Emmanuele Cassar, Zabbar
EBY 495	Bedford YMQ	Marshall	B49F	12/81	by 10/91	Alphonse Abela, (Peppin Garage), Ghaxaq
EBY 496	Bedford YRQ	Plaxton Panorama Elite III	DP45F	3/75	by 8/86	John Mary Ciappara, Birkirkara
EBY 497	Bedford YRQ	Plaxton Panorama Elite III	C45F	5/75	by 4/85	Angelo Sammit, San Giljan
EBY 498	AEC Reliance MU3RV	Aquilina (1973)	DP41F	1956	by 1/87	Christopher Caruana, Zabbar
EBY 499	Ford R1014	Duple Dominant	B45F	10/83	01/01	Jesmond Zerafa, Zejtun
EBY 500	Ford V8 f/c	Schembri (1976)	B40F	1945	by 4/76	Joseph Grech, Mqabba
EBY 501	Commer Avenger III	Aquilina	B39F	1957	by 12/91	Brian Grech, Birzebbugia
EBY 502	Bedford f/c	Brincat	B39F	unknown	by 8/75	Frank Scicluna, Zabbar

EBY 488	New
EBY 489	
EBY 490, Y-0490, DRW 908T	Tedd, Winterslow
EBY 491, Y-0491, LBR 270N	Killay, Swansea
EBY 492, Y-0492, Y-0864, Y-1564, A-2829, 2829	Unscheduled bus, Malta (Welcome Garage)
EBY 493, Y-0493, UJB 725N	Reliance, Newbury, 141
EBY 494, Y-0494, Y-1195, A-2312, 2312, 2908	Route bus, Malta
EBY 495, Y-0495, WVG 787X	Norfolk County Council
EBY 496, Y-0496, HKP 219N	West Kent, Biggin Hill
EBY 497, Y-0497, JWX 93N	Lockey, Bishop Auckland
EBY 498, Y-0498, Y-0902, Y-1602, A-2673, 2673, VWE 258	Unscheduled bus, Malta
EBY 499, A666 BDL	Isle of Wight County Council, Carisbrooke
EBY 500, Y-0500, Y-1201, A-2329, 2329, 1058	Route bus, Malta
	(This vehicle underwent refurbishment between November 1998 and August 2001, when it returned to service)
EBY 501, Y-0501, Y-0899, Y-1599, A-3441, 3441	Unscheduled bus, Malta
EBY 502, Y-0502, Y-1203, A-2337, 2337	Of Maltese origin

DBY 506 catches the evening sun, as it travels along the sea-front at Bugibba returning from Cirkewwa on route 48, on 4th August 2001.

EBY 503	Bedford YRQ	Duple Dominant I	C45F	8/75	by 11/84	Alphonse Abela, (Peppin Garage), Ghaxaq
EBY 504	Ford R1114	Duple Dominant II	C45F	5/78	1/94	Nazzareno Abela, Zejtun
EBY 505	Bedford YRQ	Plaxton Panorama Elite III Exp	C45F	3/76	by 1/87	Saviour Grech, Mqabba
EBY 506	Ford V8 f/c	Casha	B39F	1941	by 4/73	Emanuele Camilleri, Mosta
EBY 507	Diamond T f/c	Zammit	B40F	1937	by 10/54	M. A. Zammit, Qormi
EBY 508	Bedford YLQ	Duple Dominant II	C45F	3/78	by 6/89	Francis Galea, Fgura
EBY 509	Dodge f/c	Sammut	B40F	7/54	7/54	Mario Cassar, Ghaxaq
EBY 510	AEC Reliance 6MU2RA	Willowbrook	B45F	9/68	by 8/81	Carmelo k/a Charles Mifsud, Mgarr
EBY 511	Inter f/c	Schembri	B40F	unknown	by 2/91	George Micallef, Qormi
EBY 512	Bedford SB	Barbara	B40F	1956	1956	Wilfred Cardona, Marsa
EBY 513	Bedford YRQ	Plaxton Panorama Elite II	C45F	5/72	3/85	Mario Zarb, Birkirkara
EBY 514	Bedford SB	Schembri	B40F	1951	12/70	Michael Camenzuli, Zejtun
EBY 515	Bedford SB	Aquilina	B40F	unknown	by 8/86	Joseph Grech, Mqabba
EBY 516	Bedford YRQ	Duple Dominant I	C45F	1/73	by 4/85	Francis Galea, Fgura
EBY 517	Bedford SB	Brincat (1974)	B40F	1953	1/74	Paul Farrugia, Mqabba
EBY 518	Dodge f/c	Debono	B40F	unknown	by 7/73	Grezzju Grech, Zabbar
EBY 519	Bedford YRQ	Duple Dominant I	DP45F	12/72	1982	Alfred Mercieca, Marsa
EBY 520	Bristol LH6L	Eastern Coach Works	B45F	2/76	by 7/87	Victor Camilleri, Naxxar
EBY 521	Bedford YLQ	Duple Dominant II	C45F	4/77	by 8/86	Catherine Brincat, Qrendi
EBY 522	Bedford SB	Debono	B40F	1951	10/68	Spiridione Abela, Zejtun
EBY 523	Bristol LH6L	Eastern Coach Works	B45F	1/75	by 11/84	Mario & Marisa Baldacchino, Ghaxaq
EBY 524	Bristol LH6L	Eastern Coach Works	B45F	12/74	by 9/85	Francis Galea, Fgura
EBY 525	AEC Swift 4MP2R1	Park Royal	B46F	10/70	8/81	John Muscat, Mosta
EBY 526	Ford V8 n/c	Zammit	B36F	by 12/42	by 2/64	Joseph Vassallo, Siggiewi
EBY 527	Bedford YLQ	Duple Dominant II	C45F	1/78	by 8/86	Joseph Zammit, Qormi
EBY 528	Maltese Docks/Bedford	Debono	B40F	9/69	9/69	Maria Camilleri, Mgarr
EBY 529	Dodge f/c	Aquilina	B40F	11/54	11/54	Eleo Fenech, Mgarr
EBY 530	Maltese Docks/Leyland f/c	Barbara (1970)	B40F	1/59	1/59	

EBY 528, on lay-over at Saqqajja Terminus in Rabat after working route 84 to Mtarfa, and is soon to leave for Valletta, on 27th July 2001. Notice the radiator grill adorned with badges.

Bus	Registrations	Origin
EBY 503, Y-0503, KYS 415P		Burnside, Church Warsop
EBY 504, Y-0504, Y-0913, YNX 447S		Unscheduled bus, Malta
EBY 505, Y-0505, LRG 66P		Williams, Brecon
EBY 506, Y-0506, Y-1207, A-2357, 2357		Of Maltese origin
EBY 507, Y-0507, Y-1208, A-2366, 2366		n/c Route bus, Malta
EBY 508, Y-0508, GHG 115S		Wilson, Failsworth
EBY 509, Y-0509, Y-1210, A-2370, 2370		New
EBY 510, Y-0510, Y-1211, A-2374, TNY 493G		Cynon Valley, 3
EBY 511, Y-0511, Y-0919, Y-1619, A-5292, 5292		Unscheduled bus, Malta
EBY 512, Y-0512, Y-1213, A-2394, 2394		New
EBY 513, Y-0513, DDC 104K		T R Morris, Llanfyllin
EBY 514, Y-0514, Y-1215, A-2402, 2402, 2573		Ministry of Defence
EBY 515, Y-0515, Y-1622, A-3343, 3343		Of unknown origin
EBY 516, Y-0516, TYG 803L		New Enterprise, Tonbridge
EBY 517, Y-0517, Y-1218, A-2425, 2425, EMS 835		Horwood, Killin
EBY 518, Y-0518, Y-1219, A-2426, 2426		Of unknown origin
EBY 519, Y-0519, MTX 250L		Williams, Brecon
EBY 520, Y-0520, OCA 626P		Jones, Login (originally Crosville Motor Services, SLL 626)
EBY 521, Y-0521, OAN 962R		Reliance, Newbury, 152
EBY 522, Y-0522, Y-1223, A-2435, 2435		Of Egyptian origin
EBY 523, Y-0523, Y-1224, GLJ 489N		Hants and Dorset, 3557
EBY 524, Y-0524, GLJ 479N		Hants and Dorset, 3547
EBY 525, Y-0525, Y-1226, A-2442, EGN 237J		London Transport, SMS 237
EBY 526, Y-0526, Y-1227, A-2452, 2452		Of unknown origin
EBY 527, Y-0527, SJR 307S		Tompkin, Countesthorpe
EBY 528, Y-0528, Y-1229, A-2458, 2458		New
EBY 529, Y-0529, Y-1230, A-2472, 2472		New
EBY 530, Y-0530, Y-1231, A-2484, 2484		New

(*This vehicle was rebuilt both during 1954 and 1982.*)

EBY 533 is seen by the aqueduct close to the Dar tal-Providenza Home as it returns to Siggiewi from Ghar Lapsi, on the summer extension (route 94) of route 89, on Sunday 20th August 2000.

EBY 531	Dodge Kew f/c	Xurrieq	B40F	unknown	by 3/69	Philip Caruana, Zebbug
EBY 532	Ford ET7 f/c	Casha	B40F	unknown	by 4/99	Joseph Zahra, Birzebbugia
EBY 533	Maltese Docks f/c	Casha	B40F	unknown	by 8/74	Paul Borg, Mosta
EBY 534	AEC Swift 4MP2R2	MCW	B46F	4/71	by 8/81	Mario Attard, Zebbug
EBY 535	Maltese Docks/Bedford	Debono	B39F	12/56	12/56	Anthony Saliba, Zabbar
EBY 536	Dodge f/c	Casha	B40F	unknown	by 8/74	Felix Fenech, Mosta
EBY 537	Ford ET7	Zammit	B36C	by 12/52	by 8/74	Anthony Falzon, Qormi
EBY 538	Dodge f/c	Tonna	B40F	unknown	by 7/73	Ivan Zammit, Naxxar
EBY 539	Bedford YRQ	Plaxton Panorama Elite III	DP45F	7/75	by 4/85	Paul Rocco Ltd, Marsa
EBY 540	Maltese Docks f/c	Barbara	B40F	1967	1967	Filippa k/a Phylllis d'Amato, Zebbug
EBY 541	AEC Swift 4MP2R1	Park Royal	B46F	10/70	12/80	Grazio Borg, Zabbar
EBY 542	Bristol LH6L	Eastern Coach Works	B43F	11/73	by 11/84	Joseph Abdilla, Safi
EBY 543	Leyland Leopard PSU4C/4R	Plaxton Derwent	B46F	4/76	6/90	Mario Joseph Grech, Qormi
EBY 544	Bristol LH6L	Eastern Coach Works	B45F	12/74	by 8/86	Saviour Camilleri, Naxxar
EBY 545	Bedford YRQ	Duple Dominant I	C45F	7/74	4/86	Joseph Mifsud, Naxxar

EBY 531, Y-0531, Y-1232, A-2488, 2488   Of unknown origin
EBY 532, Y-0532, Y-1233, A-2489, 2489   Route bus, Malta
EBY 533, Y-0533, Y-1234, A-2490, 2490   Unknown history
EBY 534, Y-0534, Y-1235, A-2492, EGN 572J   London Transport, SMS 572
EBY 535, Y-0535, Y-1236, A-2493, 2493   New
EBY 536, Y-0536, Y-1237, A-2500, 2500   Of unknown origin
EBY 537, Y-0537, Y-1238, A-2501, 2501   Of unknown origin
EBY 538, Y-0538, Y-1239, A-2503, 2503   Route bus (n/c), Malta
EBY 539, Y-0539, JNK 559N   Plumpton Coaches
EBY 540, Y-0540, Y-1241, A-2520, 2520   New
EBY 541, Y-0541, Y-1242, A-2525, EGN 247J   London Transport, SMS 247
EBY 542, Y-0542, Y-1243, NLJ 515M   Hants & Dorset, 3515
EBY 543, Y-0543, LUG 524P   Wealden, Nettleshead
EBY 544, Y-0544, GDV 460N   Western National, 1611
EBY 545, Y-0545, STW 705M   Ron's, Ashington

EBY 559 is seen between journeys on route 27 to Marsaxlokk, at Valletta Bus Terminus on Easter Monday, 2001. It is one of the few vehicles to carry a locally-built body by Farrugia. A horse-drawn *karrozzin*, known in English as a gharry, overtakes the bus, on its way to provide rides round Valletta's narrow streets.

EBY 546	Leyland Leopard PSU4/?R	Grech	B46F	unknown	by 3/90	Nazareno Agius, Zebbug
EBY 547	Commer Avenger IV	Debono	B40F	1961	by 2/68	Silvio & Albert Camilleri, Naxxar
EBY 548	Bedford SBO	Barbara	B40F	7/55	7/55	Martin Chetchuti, Mgarr
EBY 549	Bedford QL	Brincat	B40F	unknown	by 9/73	Victor Grech, Mosta
EBY 550	Bedford YRQ	Plaxton Panorama Elite II	DP45F	2/72	by 11/84	Paul Rocco (Marsa) Ltd, Zabbar
EBY 551	Maltese Docks f/c	Ciantar	B45F	by 12/69	by 8/74	Carmel Cutajar, Paola
EBY 552	Bedford f/c	Tonna	B40F	unknown	by 8/75	Joseph Caruana, Tarxien
EBY 553	Bedford f/c	Aquilina	B40F	unknown	12/58	John Ciappara, Qormi
EBY 554	AEC Swift 4MP2R	Marshall	B46F	4/70	by 5/91	Alex Pulo, Paola
EBY 555	AEC Mercury GM4RH	Brincat	B40F	1957	11/67	George Casha, Qormi
EBY 556	Maltese Docks/AEC	Aquilina	B40F	10/63	10/63	Carmelo k/a Charles Farrugia, Fgura
EBY 557	Leyland f/c	Casha	B45F	1954	by 5/95	Mario Farrugia, Mqabba
EBY 558	Bedford YLQ	Plaxton Panorama Elite III	DP45F	11/76	by 10/86	Paul Rocco (Marsa Ltd), Zabbar
EBY 559	AEC Mercury	Farrugia	B40F	1961	by 10/87	Carmel Cachia, Ghaxaq
EBY 560	Bedford f/c	Tonna	B40F	unknown	by 2/68	Joseph Camilleri, Rabat

EBY 546, Y-0546	Of unknown origin
EBY 547, Y-0547, Y-1248, A-2543, 2543	Of unknown origin
EBY 548, Y-0548, Y-1249, A-2545, 2545	New
EBY 549, Y-0549, Y-1250, A-2550, 2550	Of unknown origin
EBY 550, Y-0550, Y-1251, WCF 539F	Morley, West Row
EBY 551, Y-0551, Y-1252, A-2554, 2554	Of unknown origin
EBY 552, Y-0552, Y-1253, A-2558, 2558	Of unknown origin
EBY 553, Y-0553, Y-1254, A-2561, 2561	Of unknown origin
EBY 554, Y-0554, Y-0633, Y-1334, A-2881, AML 16H	Route bus, Malta (originally London Transport, SM 16)
EBY 555, Y-0555, Y-1256, A-2570, 2570, 4592	Lorry
EBY 556, Y-0556, Y-1257, A-2571, 2571	New
EBY 557, Y-0557	*(Further details cannot be verified)*
EBY 558, Y-0558, NVA 48R	Miller, Foxton
EBY 559, Y-0559, Y-0900, Y-1600, A-2899, 2899	Unscheduled bus, Malta
EBY 560, Y-0560, Y-1261, A-2853, 2853	Unknown

EBY 572 is seen at Qawra Bus Terminus on April 20th 2000, prior to returning to Valletta on route 49. The distinctive flashes adorning its headlights and direction indicators are clearly in view. The Sammut bodywork is completed in the islands, Sammut being one of several local coachbuilders.

EBY 561	Bedford f/c	Debono	B45F	1968	by 11/98	Natasha Sammut, Gzira
EBY 562	*This registration number is currently not in use.*					Horace Vella, Qormi
EBY 563	Bedford YRQ	Plaxton Elite Express II	DP45F	5/72	by 7/88	John Ciappara, Qormi
EBY 564	AEC Swift 4MP2R1	Park Royal/Busuttil (2001)	B46F	10/70	8/80	Saviour k/a Silvio Sammut, San Gwann
EBY 565	Maltese Docks f/c	Gauci	B40F	12/62	12/62	George Valletta, Qormi
EBY 566	Bedford YLQ	Duple Dominant II	C45F	4/77	5/85	Paul Farrugia, Zurrieq
EBY 567	AEC Reliance 2MU3RA	Grech	B45F	1959	by 5/95	Victor Mifsud, Mgarr
EBY 568	Ford R1014	Duple Dominant IA	C45F	7/78	4/86	Tressi Azzopardi, Attard
EBY 569	Ford 570E	Zammit	B41F	1962	by 12/72	Joseph Grech, Mqabba
EBY 570	Ford ET7	Sammut	B36F	by 12/54	by 8/74	Saviour Zahra, Rabat
EBY 571	Bedford QL	Barbara	B40F	unknown	11/62	Gerald Sultana, Santa Venera
EBY 572	Federal f/c	Sammut	B40F	1945	by 8/74	John Mary Camilleri, Naxxar
EBY 573	Bedford YRQ	Plaxton Panorama Elite III	C45F	10/73	by 9/85	Saviour k/a Silvio Sammut, San Gwann
EBY 574	*This registration number is currently not in use*					Gerald Sultana, Cospicua

EBY 561, Y-0685, Y-0866, Y-1566, A-7053, 7053   Route bus, Malta
EBY 562
EBY 563, Y-0563, CJR 823K   Woodcock, Buxton
EBY 564, Y-0564, Y-1265, A-2589, EGN 268J   London Transport, SMS 268
        (*This vehicle was extensively rebodied by Paul Busuttil*
        between May 1998 and March 2001)
EBY 565, Y-0565, Y-1266, A-2590, 2590   New
EBY 566, Y-0566, RAW 14R   Evans, Penrhyncoch
EBY 567, Y-0567, Y-0861, Y-1561, 9191 NW   Unscheduled bus, Malta
EBY 568, Y-0568, NJS 622S   Pemberton, Upton
EBY 569, Y-0569, Y-1270, A-2595, 2595   Of unknown origin
EBY 570, Y-0570, Y-1271, A-2596, 2596   Of unknown origin
EBY 571, Y-0571, Y-1272, A-2599, 2599   Of unknown origin
EBY 572, Y-0572, Y-1273, A-2600, 2600   Of unknown origin
EBY 573, Y-0573, OPT 730M   Ross, Cotgrave
EBY 574

EBY 584 awaits further service on route 652 to Golden Bay from Sliema Ferry on 29th July 2001.

EBY 575	Maltese Docks/Leyland f/c	Schembri	B40F	unknown	by 8/74	Kevin Debono, Gzira
EBY 576	AEC Swift 4MP2R	Park Royal	B46F	4/70	2/81	Andrew Garnisi, Luqa
EBY 577	Bedford YLQ	Plaxton Elite Express III	C45F	5/77	by 11/85	Paul Rocco (Marsa Ltd), Marsa
EBY 578	Mercedes OP/R	Sammut	B36F	1949	by 9/85	Gerald Sultana, Cospicua
EBY 579	Bedford SB8	Sammut	B40F	1/59	1/59	Jason Azzopardi, Bormla
EBY 580	Bedford YRQ	Plaxton Panorama Elite III	C45F	5/73	by 11/84	Silvio Schembri, Qormi
EBY 581	Bedford f/c	Barbara	B39F	unknown	2/58	Joseph Borg, Qormi
EBY 582	Ford ET7	Sammut	B36F	by 12/54	by 5/74	Silvio Borg, Mellieha
EBY 583	Bedford YLQ	Plaxton Panorama Elite III	C45F	5/77	by 2/88	Mario Bonavia, Naxxar
EBY 584	Maltese Docks f/c	Farrugia	B40F	1966	1966	Stephen Cilia, Gharghur
EBY 585	Bedford YRQ	Duple Dominant I	C45F	9/74	by 1/86	Spiridione Pulo, Santa Venera
EBY 586	Bedford SB	Casha	B40F	1952	by 8/74	Carmel Borg, Rabat
EBY 587	Bedford YRQ	Plaxton Panorama Elite III	DP45F	1/73	by 11/84	Winstin Muscat, San Pawl il-Bahar
EBY 588	Ford V8 f/c	Zammit	B39F	1945	by 3/73	Silvio Borg, Mellieha
EBY 589	AEC Swift 4MP2R1	Park Royal	B46F	1/71	by 10/81	Charles Sant, Mellieha

EBY 575, Y-0575, Y-1276, A-2620, 2620	Of unknown origin
EBY 576, Y-0576, Y-1277, A-2621, AML 60H	London Transport, SMD 60
EBY 577, Y-0577, OHY 790R	Thomas, Barry
EBY 578, Y-0578, Y-0691, A-4756, 4756	Route bus, Malta
EBY 579, Y-0579, Y-1280, A-2630, 2630	New
EBY 580, Y-0580, Y-1281, XWW 791L	Morley, West Row
EBY 581, Y-0581, Y-1282, A-2638, 2638	Of unknown origin
EBY 582, Y-0582, Y-1283, A-2658, 2658	Of unknown origin
EBY 583, Y-0583, WTU 123R	Brownrigg & Cook, Egremont
EBY 584, Y-0584, Y-1285, A-2676, 2676	New
EBY 585, Y-0585, RAL 968N	Cooper, Killamarsh
EBY 586, Y-0586, Y-1287, A-2705, 2705	Ministry of Supply
EBY 587, Y-0587, Y-1288, CNT 265L	Williams, Brecon
EBY 588, Y-0588, Y-1289, A-2708, 2708	Route bus (n/c), Malta
EBY 589, Y-0589, Y-1290, A-2709, EGN 292J	London Transport, SMS 292

EBY 612 waits in Qrendi before returning to Valletta on route 38 on 24th August 2000. The imposing Church of St Mary overlooks the bus terminus in the village.

EBY 590	Maltese Docks/AEC f/c	Debono	B40F	10/68	10/68	Gaetano Fenech, Zejtun
EBY 591	Bedford YLQ	Plaxton Panorama Elite III	C45F	3/77	by 10/87	Victor Spiteri, Birkirkara
EBY 592	Bristol LH6L	Eastern Coach Works	B45F	2/76	by 10/86	Natasha Sammut, Gzira
EBY 593	Bedford YRQ	Duple Dominant I	DP45F	3/75	by 9/85	Carmelo Muscat, Naxxar
EBY 594	Bedford YRQ	Duple Dominant I	C45F	9/74	1/85	Albert Sammut, San Gwann
EBY 595	Ford R1014	Duple Dominant	B46F	12/78	8/91	Owen Spiteri, Mqabba
EBY 596	Bedford YRQ	Duple Dominant I Express	C45F	10/75	by 11/84	Michael Camenzuli, Marsascala
EBY 597	Bedford YRQ	Plaxton Panorama Elite III	DP45F	4/75	by 8/86	Grace Camilleri, Zabbar
EBY 598	Bedford QL	Vella	B36F	1945	by 7/55	Philip Caruana, Zebbug
EBY 599	Bedford YRQ	Plaxton Panorama Elite III	C45F	9/74	by 1/86	Carmel Abela, Zejtun
EBY 600	Ford 570E	Aquilina	B40F	1963	3/74	Filippa k/a Phyllis d'Amato, Zebbug
EBY 601	Dodge f/c	Sammut	B39F	1944	by 9/69	Gerald Sultana, San Gwann
EBY 602	Dodge f/c	Casha	B36F	by 12/35	by 8/74	Joseph Saliba, Zabbar
EBY 603	International Harvester f/c	Tonna	B40F	unknown	by 8/74	Michael Spiteri, Fgura
EBY 604	Ford R1014	Plaxton Panorama Elite III	C45F	3/75	by 4/85	Walter Camilleri, Qormi
EBY 605	Bedford YLQ	Plaxton Panorama Elite III	C45F	3/77	by 2/88	John Borg, Rabat
EBY 606	Bedford YLQ	Duple Dominant II	C45F	2/79	by 5/95	Louis Borg, Mellieha
EBY 607	Bedford YRQ	Plaxton Panorama Elite III	DP45F	10/74	by 4/90	Paul Mifsud, Mellieha
EBY 608	Bedford YRQ	Plaxton Panorama Elite III Exp	C45F	8/75	by 10/87	Charles Schembri, Qormi
EBY 609	Bedford YLQ	Plaxton Panorama Elite III	C45F	8/76	by 10/87	Grazio Borg, Zabbar
EBY 610	Bedford YLQ	Duple Dominant I	DP45F	5/76	4/86	John Cauchi, Mellieha
EBY 611	Bristol LH6L	Plaxton Panorama Elite III Exp	C45F	11/77	by 5/90	Joseph Xuereb, Mellieha
EBY 612	AEC f/c	Debono (1971)	B43F	unknown	by 4/90	Charles Farrugia, Mqabba
EBY 613	Maltese Docks f/c	Barbara	B40F	9/66	9/66	Saviour Zammit, Tarxien
EBY 614	Bedford YRQ	Duple Dominant I	C45F	1/75	by 7/87	Anthony Camilleri, Qormi
EBY 615	Bedford YRQ	Plaxton Elite II Express	C45F	5/76	by 1/85	Martin Bartolo, Mosta
EBY 616	Maltese Docks f/c	Barbara	B40F	3/70	3/70	Marco Magro, Mqabba
EBY 617	*This registration is currently not in use.*					Paul Buttigieg, Zabbar
EBY 618	Bedford SB	Barbara (1971)	B43F	unknown	3/71	George Buhagiar, Mosta
EBY 619	Ford R1014	Willowbrook	B46F	1978	by 2/92	Andrew Abela, Zejtun
EBY 620	*This registration is currently not in use.*					Manuel Cassar, Zabbar

EBY 592 and EBY 520 are Bristol LHs, both originally delivered to the Crosville fleet in early 1976. It is interesting to compare the frontal treatment of each vehicle now, especially concerning the unique application of the orange band on 592. Once again the scene is Valletta Bus Terminus, and both vehicles are working route 62 to Sliema, on 24th August 2000.

EBY 590, Y-0590, Y-1291, A-2714, 2714	New
EBY 591, Y-0591, PET 214R	Halliday Hartle, Buxton
EBY 592, Y-0592, OCA 635P	Jones, Login (originally Crosville Motor Services, SLL 635)
EBY 593, Y-0593, HNT 841N	Day, Abertillery
EBY 594, Y-0594, SMR 622N	Tourist, Figheldean
EBY 595, Y-0595, COO 242T	Suffolk County Council, Ipswich
EBY 596, Y-0596, Y-1297, KBX 39P	Davies Bros., Pencader, 99
EBY 597, Y-0597, HMV 645N	Ron's, Ashington
	(*This vehicle has been heavily rebuilt since June 2000*)
EBY 598, Y-0598, Y-1299, A-2789, 2789	Of unknown origin
EBY 599, Y-0599, SJR 426N	Holmes, Clay Cross
EBY 600, Y-0600, Y-1301, A-2804, 2804, 8557	Convent, St Julian's
EBY 601, Y-0601, Y-1302, A-2806, 2806	Route bus (n/c), Malta
EBY 602, Y-0602, Y-1303, A-2813, 2813	Route bus (n/c), Malta
EBY 603, Y-0603, Y-1304, A-2814, 2814	Of unknown origin
EBY 604, Y-0604, JDS 644N	Taylor, Derby
EBY 605, Y-0605, TWT 504R	Evans, Tregaron
EBY 606, Y-0606, DTM 958T	Williams, Brecon
EBY 607, Y-0607, Y-0431, Y-1132, UUP 3N	Route bus, Malta
EBY 608, Y-0608, KDF 856P	Pulham, Bourton on the Water
EBY 609, Y-0609, SUP 436R	Chivers, Elstead
EBY 610, Y-0610, ODU 251P	Sayer, Ipswich
EBY 611, Y-0611, RDE 298S	Williams, Brecon
EBY 612, Y-0612, Y-0915, Y-1615, A-208, 208	Unscheduled bus, Malta
EBY 613, Y-0613, Y-1314, A-2835, 2835	New
EBY 614, Y-0614, GUX 949N	Rees, Llanelly Hill
EBY 615, Y-0615, Y-1316, NTO 34P	Leiston Motor Hire
EBY 616, Y-0616, Y-1317, A-2838, 2838	New
EBY 617	
EBY 618, Y-0618, Y-1319, A-2840, 2840	Of unknown origin
EBY 619, Y-0619, XKX 856S	Hampton, London SE1
EBY 620	

EBY 625 pauses at Ghadira Bay, Mellieha on route 45 to Cirkewwa on 14th April 2001. Of a total of fifty-seven AEC Swifts imported to the island, fifty-six entered service either as route buses or with the MINISTERU TA' L-EDUKAZZJONI. These latter now number fifteen in a purple and white livery.

EBY 621	*This registration is currently not in use.*					Carmel Farrugia, Fgura
EBY 622	Leyland Royal Tiger PSU1/16	Aquilina (1975)	B44F	6/53	by 6/90	Joseph Busuttil, Zabbar
EBY 623	*This registration is currently not in use.*					Francis Said, Zejtun
EBY 624	Bedford YRQ	Duple Dominant I Express	C45F	8/75	by 2/88	Paul Buttigieg, Zabbar
EBY 625	AEC Swift 4MP2R	Marshall	B46F	1/70	12/80	Michael Spiteri, Qrendi
EBY 626	Bedford YLQ	Plaxton Panorama Elite III Exp	C45F	7/77	by 4/85	Pacifico Scerri, Mosta
EBY 627	Bedford f/c	Debono	B40F	unknown	by 8/74	Carmelo Cassar, Mqabba
EBY 628	Maltese Docks/AEC f/c	Barbara	B40F	1964	by 12/79	George Micallef, Qormi
EBY 629	Commer Avenger IV	Debono	DP40F	1968	4/90	Gerald Sultana, Santa Venera
EBY 630	Bedford YLQ	Plaxton Panorama Elite III	C45F	8/78	by 3/90	Mario Farrugia, Attard
EBY 631	Dodge T110 f/c	Casha	B39F	unknown	by 1/86	John Brincat, Fgura
EBY 632	Bedford SB	Zammit	B36F	unknown	by 4/69	Joseph Demanuele, Hamrun
EBY 633	AEC Swift 4MP2R2	MCW	B46F	5/71	by 5/92	Stephen Cilia, Gharghur

EBY 621
EBY 622, Y-0622, Y-0883, Y-1583, A-5571, 5571, FCK 433   Unscheduled bus, Malta
EBY 623
EBY 624, Y-0624, JDK 500P   Ouse Valley, Goldington
EBY 625, Y-0625, Y-1326, A-2862, AML 8H   London Transport, SM 8
EBY 626, Y-0626, Y-1327, CAA 840R   Tedd, Thruxton
EBY 627, Y-0627, Y-1328, A-2864, 2864   Of unknown origin
EBY 628, Y-0628, Y-1329, A-2870, 2870   Of unknown origin
EBY 629, Y-0629, Y-0896, Y-1596, A-3334, 3334   Unscheduled bus, Malta
EBY 630, Y-0630, UFT 912T   Briggs, Swansea
EBY 631, Y-0631, 2128   Unscheduled bus, Malta
EBY 632, Y-0632, Y-1333, A-2879, 2879   Of unknown origin
EBY 633. Y-0633, Y-0554, Y-1255, A-2566, EGN 603J   Route bus, Malta, (originally London Transport, SMS 603)
        (This vehicle was refurbished between April 1998 and
        April 1999, and then between September 1999 and April 2000)

FBY 646 had been on Malta for only two months, when seen at San Gwann on route 41 on 28th March 2002. S

EBY 634	AEC Swift 4MP2R1	Marshall	B46F	3/71	by 8/81	Paul Zammit. Tarxien
EBY 635	Bedford f/c	Ciantar	B40F	unknown	1972	Tommy Borg, Mellieha
EBY 636	Ford V8 n/c	Gasan	B40F	1945	1950	Joseph Borg, Zabbar
EBY 637	Leyland Tiger Cub PSUC1/13	East Lancs	B45F	1967	by 8/81	Albert Camilleri, Naxxar
EBY 638	Bedford SB	Tonna	B40F	by 3/69	by 3/69	Raymond Aquilina, Gwardmangia
EBY 639	Federal f/c	Aquilina	B40F	5/55	by 8/74	John Caruana, Mosta
EBY 640	Bedford SB3	Casha	B40F	6/58	6/58	Dominic Borg, Mellieha
FBY 641	AEC Swift 4MP2R1	Marshall	B46F	9/71	by 8/81	Emanuel Borg, Birkirkara
FBY 642	AEC Swift 4MP2R1	Park Royal	B46F	10/70	2/82	Brian Grech, Birzebbugia
FBY 643	Bedford YLQ	Plaxton Panorama Elite III	C45F	3/77	by 9/85	Angelo Spiteri, Ghaxaq
FBY 644	Bedford SB	Brincat	B40F	unknown	by 7/73	Reuben Borg, Mellieha
FBY 645	Bedford SB	Aquilina	B40F	1952	3/70	Paul Rocco, Marsa
FBY 646	Bedford YMP	Marshall	B48F	11/83	1/02	John Caruana, Mosta
FBY 647	AEC Regal 0662	Debono	B40F	1938	by 12/60	Emmanuele Cortis, Naxxar

EBY 634, Y-0634, Y-1335, A-2882, EGN 212J   London Transport, SMS 212
(*This vehicle was rebuilt between 1991 and 1994*)
EBY 635, Y-0635, Y-1336, A-2889, 2889   Of unknown origin
EBY 636, Y-0636, Y-1337, A-2890, 2890   Of unknown origin
EBY 637, Y-0637, Y-1338, A-2895, GBV 13E   Blackburn, 13
EBY 638, Y-0638, Y-1339, A-2900, 2900   New
EBY 639, Y-0639, Y-1340, A-2920, 2920, 3293   Route bus, Malta
EBY 640, Y-0640, Y-1341, A-2922, 2922   New
FBY 641, Y-0641, Y-1342, A-2925, EGN 202J   London Transport, SMS 202
FBY 642, Y-0642, Y-1343, EGN 243J   London Transport, SMS 243
FBY 643, Y-0643, MPX 7R   Bell, Winterslow
FBY 644, Y-0644, Y-1345, A-2958, 2958   Of unknown origin
FBY 645, Y-0645, Y-1346, A-2980, 2980   Ministry of Supply
FBY 646, A203 LCL   Lewis, Llanrhystyd
FBY 647, Y-0647, Y-1348, A-2983, 2983, ERA 914   Midland General, 126

FBY 662 was repainted in the summer of 2001 in a deeper shade of yellow than normal. It is seen negotiating the roundabout near Pieta Creek on route 49 from Qawra on 6th August 2001.

FBY 648	Ford ET7 f/c	Aquilina	B40F	1/57	by 10/87	Anthony Schembri, Qormi
FBY 649	Dodge f/c	Casha	B40F	unknown	by 4/64	Charles Seychell, Fgura
FBY 650	Bedford YLQ	Duple Dominant I	DP45F	5/76	by 9/85	Kristinu Pace, Qormi
FBY 651	Bedford YRQ	Plaxton Panorama Elite II	DP45F	3/71	by 1/85	Alfred Mercieca, Marsa
FBY 652	Bedford YRQ	Duple Dominant I	C45F	5/75	by 5/95	Franco Camilleri, Santa Venera
FBY 653	Dodge Kew	Barbara	B36F	by 5/60	by 5/60	Alexander Schembri, Qormi
FBY 654	Bedford YRQ	Plaxton Panorama Elite II	C45F	5/72	by 9/85	Albert Sammut, San Gwann
FBY 655	Bedford YRQ	Plaxton Panorama Elite II	C45F	4/72	by 4/90	Francis Galea, Fgura
FBY 656	AEC Swift 4MP2R	Marshall	B46F	2/70	by 4/94	Anthony Darmanin, Zabbar
FBY 657	Bedford YMQ	Marshall	B49F	12/81	by 2/92	Andrew Abela, Zejtun
FBY 658	Leyland Comet 14SC	Aquilina (1967)	B40F	1963	1/67	Paul Rocco, Tarxien
FBY 659	AEC Mustang GM6RH	Aquilina (1968)	B40F	unknown	by 8/86	Paul Axiaq, Bugibba
FBY 660	Bedford YLQ	Duple Dominant II	C45F	10/78	by 1/87	Grezzju Caruana, Zabbar
FBY 661	Willys D n/c	Brincat	B34F	unknown	by 4/90	Rosaria Falzon, Fgura
FBY 662	AEC Swift 4MP2R	Marshall	B46F	2/70	8/80	Emmanuele Caruana, Gharghur

FBY 648, Y-0648, Y-0867, Y-1567, A-5575, 5575		Unscheduled bus, Malta
FBY 649, Y-0649, Y-1350, A-2992, 2992		Ministry of Supply
FBY 650, Y-0650, MTX 661P		Rees, Llanelly Hill
FBY 651, Y-0651, HWW 60J		Williams, Brecon
FBY 652, Y-0652, JAP 441N		Camden, Sevenoaks
FBY 653, Y-0653, Y-1354, A-3032, 3032		New
FBY 654, Y-0654, RPR 740K		Adams, Handley
FBY 655, Y-0655, Y-0657, UNU178K		Route bus, Malta
FBY 656, Y-0656, Y-0321, Y-1022, A-0358, AML14H		Route bus, Malta (originally, London Transport, SM 14)
FBY 657, Y-0657, WVG788X		Norfolk County Council
FBY 658, Y-0658, Y-1359, A-3063, 3063		Lorry chassis
FBY 659, Y-0659, Y-0884		
FBY 660, Y-0660, ANR 743T		Cropper, Leeds
FBY 661, Y-0661, Y-0857, Y-1557, A-3036, 3036, 2219		Unscheduled bus, Malta
FBY 662, Y-0662, Y-1363, A-3075, AML 33H		London Transport, SM 33

FBY 671 awaits attention at Kirkop on 30th July 2001.

FBY 663	Bedford f/c	Barbara (1960)	B40F	by 2/63	by 6/90	Consiglio Gatt, Qormi
FBY 664	Reo f/c	Aquilina	B36F	4/34	4/34	Joseph Scerri, Mosta
FBY 665	*This registration is currently not in use.*					Francis Galea, Fgura
FBY 666	Leyland Comet 14SC	Barbara	B40F	5/70	5/70	Joseph Scicluna, Mellieha
FBY 667	Bedford SB	Barbara	B45F	1955	5/64	Anthony Xuereb, Gharghur
FBY 668	Dodge f/c	Vella	B40F	unknown	by 8/74	Carmel Farrugia, Zabbar
FBY 669	Bedford SB	Brincat	DP41F	1959	9/92	Lorenza Caruana, Zabbar
FBY 670	Bedford YLQ	Duple Dominant II	C45F	7/77	by 7/87	Emanuel Valletta, Qormi
FBY 671	Bedford f/c	Barbara	B40F	unknown	by 4/69	Gordon Callus, Kirkop
FBY 672	Maltese Docks f/c	Brincat	B40F	3/69	3/69	Sebastian Mifsud, Mellieha
FBY 673	Bedford YLQ	Duple Dominant IA	C45F	4/77	4/86	Noel Desira, Zabbar
FBY 674	AEC Reliance 2MU3RA	Ciantar	B45F	1961	by 6/89	John Spiteri, Qormi
FBY 675	AEC Swift 4MP2R	Marshall	B46F	2/70	2/81	Dolores Muscat, Siggiewi
FBY 676	AEC Reliance MU3RV	Aquilina	B45F	6/57	by 4/93	Emanuel Buhagiar, Mosta
FBY 677	*This registration is currently not in use.*					Alfred Mercieca, Marsa

FBY 663, Y-0663, Y-0851, Y-1551, A-896, 896   Unscheduled bus, Malta
FBY 664, Y-0664, Y-1365, A-3080, 3080   New
FBY 665
FBY 666, Y-0666, Y-1367, A-3082, 3082   New
FBY 667, Y-0667, Y-1368, A-3083, 3083   Ministry of Supply
FBY 668, Y-0668, Y-1369, A-3092, 3092   Of unknown origin
FBY 669, Y-0669, Y-0911, Y-1611, A-2674, 2674   Unscheduled bus, Malta
FBY 670, Y-0670, RAW 44R   Rees, Llanelly Hill
FBY 671, Y-0671, Y-1372, A-3097, 3097   Of unknown origin
FBY 672, Y-0672, Y-1373, A-3098, 3098   New
FBY 673, Y-0673, OAN 963R   Reliance, Newbury, 153
FBY 674, Y-0674, Y-0870, Y-1570, RDB 847   Unscheduled bus, Malta (originally North Western, 847)
FBY 675, Y-0675, Y-1376, A-3114, AML 11H   London Transport, SM 11
FBY 676, Y-0676, Y-0877, Y-1577, A-4398, 4398, YKR 234   Unscheduled bus, Malta
FBY 677

FBY 686 awaits more passengers at Popeye Village, near Mellieha, on 3rd August 1999.

FBY 678	Bedford SB	Aquilina	B40F	1962	1962	Francis Caruana, Fgura
FBY 679	AEC Mercury 2GM4RA	Brincat	B40F	unknown	c10/73	Paul Buttigieg, Zabbar
FBY 680	Dodge f/c	Sammut	B40F	unknown	by 2/54	M. A. Zammit, Qormi
FBY 681	Bedford QLD	Debono	B40F	1945	1979	Paul Rocco, Marsa
FBY 682	Bedford YRQ	Duple Dominant I	C45F	1973	by 4/85	Anthony Schembri, Qormi
FBY 683	Bedford YMT	Plaxton Supreme III	C45F	4/77	by 10/86	Gerald Bugeja, Mqabba
FBY 684	Bedford QL	Casha	B40F	unknown	by 8/74	Mario Sultana, Cospicua
FBY 685	Maltese Docks f/c	Debono	B45F	1968	by 5/97	Raymond Gialanze, Zabbar
FBY 686	Ford V8 f/c	Casha (1969)	B40F	1949	by 4/69	Raymond Borg, Mellieha
FBY 687	Bedford SB	Brincat	B40F	1955	7/56	Anthony Cassar, Zabbar
FBY 688	Bedford SB	Brincat	B40F	unknown	by 4/64	Joseph Pace, Qrendi
FBY 689	Bedford YLQ	Duple Dominant I	DP45F	2/77	by 10/86	Alfred Farrugia, Mqabba
FBY 690	Bedford YRQ	Plaxton Panorama Elite III	C45F	6/75	by 1/86	Derran Cassar, Zabbar
FBY 691	Bedford YRQ	Plaxton Panorama Elite II	C45F	4/71	by 4/85	Gerald Sultana, Santa Venera

FBY 678, Y-0678, Y-1379, A-3129, 3129   New
FBY 679, Y-0679, Y-1380, A-3132, 3132, 1788   Route bus, Malta
FBY 680, Y-0680, Y-1381, A-3135, 3135   Of unknown origin
FBY 681, Y-0681, Y-1382, A-3171, 3440   Route bus, Malta
FBY 682, Y-0682, BUX 239L   Glyn Williams, Lower Tumble
FBY 683, ACY 912, Y-0912, STA 259R   Unscheduled bus, Malta
FBY 684, Y-0684, Y-1385, A-3175, 3175   Of unknown origin
FBY 685, Y-0685, Y-0893, Y-1593   Unscheduled bus, Malta
FBY 686, Y-0686, Y-1387, A-3183, 3183, 2625, 3335   Route bus, Malta
FBY 687, Y-0687, Y-1388, A-3190, 3190   Of unknown origin
FBY 688, Y-0688, Y-1389, A-3196, 3196   Of unknown origin
FBY 689, Y-0689, YAA 260R   Marchwood, Totton
FBY 690, Y-0690, KAC 440N   Letham, Dunfermline
FBY 691, Y-0691, URO 849J   Morley, West Row

FBY 702 had returned to service after its rebuild only a few weeks earlier when seen on lay-over at Valletta Bus Terminus on 10th April 2001.

FBY 692	Bedford YRQ	Duple Dominant I	C45F	1/74	by 3/86	John Abela, Zejtun
FBY 693	Bedford YRQ	Duple Dominant I	C45F	4/74	by 4/85	Stefan Sammut, San Gwann
FBY 694	Bedford SBG	Grech	B45F	1956	9/80	John Camilleri, Naxxar
FBY 695	Ford 6 f/c	Barbara	B40F	by 12/45	1959	Emmanuel Ellul, Santa Venera
FBY 696	Bedford f/c	Aquilina	B43F	unknown	10/73	George Borg, Naxxar
FBY 697	*This registration is currently not in use.*					Angelo Sammut, San Gwann
FBY 698	Leyland f/c	Aquilina (1954)	B46F	unknown	2/54	Albert Sammut, San Gwann
FBY 699	Bedford SB	Aquilina (1955)	B40F	c1954	by 3/87	Albert Camilleri, Naxxar
FBY 700	Bedford YRQ	Plaxton Panorama Elite III	DP44F	1/73	by 4/85	Angelo Muscat, Zebbug
FBY 701	Bedford f/c	Brincat	B40F	unknown	by 10/87	Michael Psaila, Siggiewi
FBY 702	Leyland Hippo	Cassar (2000)	B45F	unknown	by 7/54	Emmanuele Cassar, Zabbar
FBY 703	GMC f/c	Brincat	B40F	unknown	by 2/68	Paul Rocco, Marsa
FBY 704	Austin K4	Brincat	B36F	12/53	12/53	Joseph Ellul, Mqabba
FBY 705	Indiana f/c	Barbara (1958)	B40F	unknown	by 11/95	Silvio Muscat, Birkirkara

FBY 692, Y-0692, YAB 600M	Down, Mary Tavy
FBY 693, Y-0693, VPF 41M	Fale, Coombe Down
FBY 694, Y-0694, Y-1395, A-3225, 3225	Ministry of Supply
FBY 695, Y-0695, Y-1396, A-3230, 3230, 2484	Route bus, Malta
FBY 696, Y-0696, Y-1397, A-3231, 3231, 3132	Route bus, Malta
FBY 697	
FBY 698, Y-0698, Y-1399, A-3240, 3240	Of unknown origin
FBY 699, Y-0699, Y-0860, Y-1560, A-0354, 354	Unscheduled bus, Malta
FBY 700, Y-0700, Y-1401, UWX 113L	McLaughlin, Penwortham
FBY 701, Y-0701, Y-0855, Y-1555, A-7243, 7243	Unscheduled bus, Malta
FBY 702, Y-0702, Y-1403, A-3249, 3249	Of unknown origin
(This vehicle carried a Tonna body until being rebuilt between April 1997 and October 2000)	
FBY 703, Y-0703, Y-1404, A-3251, 3251	Of unknown origin
FBY 704, Y-0704, Y-1405, A-3252, 3252	New
FBY 705, Y-0705, Y-0360, Y-0914, Y-1614, A-2092, 2092	Route bus, Malta

FBY 708 is seen at the terminus of route 91 in Qormi on 27th March 2002, with many distinctive balconies on the houses clearly in view.

FBY 706	Bedford YRQ	Plaxton Panorama Elite III	C45F	5/73	by 3/85	Nicholas Micallef, Qormi
FBY 707	Leyland Tiger Cub PSUC1/1	Debono (1977)	B45F	1958	by 4/86	Gerald Sultana, Santa Venera
FBY 708	Bedford YRQ	Marshall	B45F	7/75	by 6/89	Justin Borg, Attard
FBY 709	Bedford SB	Barbara	B40F	12/59	12/59	Joseph Galea, Qormi
FBY 710	Ford 7V	Debono	B40F	unknown	by 9/74	Paul Sant, Mosta
FBY 711	Inter f/c	Aquilina (1949)	B40F	by 12/33	by 5/90	Carmel Farrugia, Fgura
FBY 712	*This registration is currently not in use.*					Gerald Sultana, Santa Venera
FBY 713	Dodge f/c	Zammit	B40F	unknown	by 8/74	Joseph Demanuele, Hamrun
FBY 714	Bristol LH6L	Eastern Coach Works	B45F	1/75	1/85	Anthony Attard, Rabat
FBY 715	Bedford YRQ	Duple Dominant I	DP41F	8/74	by 11/84	Rosaria Falzon, Fgura
FBY 716	Leyland Lion TS	Aquilina (1958)	B40F	by 12/39	11/58	Anthony Sant, Mellieha
FBY 717	Bedford YRQ	Plaxton Panorama Elite III	DP45F	11/71	by 4/85	Grazio Borg, Zabbar
FBY 718	*This registration is currently not in use.*					Alfred Mercieca, Marsa
FBY 719	Bedford f/c	Brincat	B39F	1964	by 7/93	John Zammit, Qormi
FBY 720	Maltese Docks f/c	Schembri	B40F	unknown	by 10/88	Charles Farrugia, Fgura

FBY 706, Y-0706, Y-1407, PGW 638L
FBY 707, Y-0707, Y-0889, Y-1589, A-3073, 3073, NHE 133

FBY 708, Y-0708, HGM 614N
FBY 709, Y-0709, Y-1410, A-3268, 3268
FBY 710, Y-0710, Y-1411, A-3270, 3270, 172
FBY 711, Y-0711, Y-0630, Y-1331, A-2877, 2877
FBY 712
FBY 713, Y-0713, Y-1414, A-3276, 3276
FBY 714, Y-0714, Y-1415, GLJ 485N
FBY 715, FBY 780, FBY 715, Y-0715, RUX 278N
FBY 716, Y-0716, Y-1417, A-3280, 3280
FBY 717, Y-0717, JTD 615K
FBY 718
FBY 719, Y-0719, Y-1420, A-3284, 3284
FBY 720, Y-0720, Y-0916, Y-1616, A-2790, 2790

Kirkbright, Colne
Aquilina, Msida (*As late as March 2002, this vehicle still carried its Y-0707 registration!*)
Atomic Weapons Research Establishment, Aldermaston
New
Route bus, Malta
Route bus, Malta

Of unknown origin
Hants and Dorset, 3553
Parfitt's, Rhymney Bridge
Unknown UK operator
Morley, West Row

Of unknown origin
Unscheduled bus, Malta

Indicative of the approaching new order of buses on the island is the front of the new Volvo/Scarnif route bus, FBY 727, seen at Scarnif's premises on 25th March 2002.

FBY 721	Bedford f/c	Brincat	B40F	unknown	by 8/74	Francis Saverio Said, Zejtun
FBY 722	Bedford YMQ	Marshall	B46F	10/80	by 5/92	Carmel Abela, Zejtun
FBY 723	AEC Swift 4MP2R5	MCW	B46F	1/72	6/80	Mario Sultana, Bormla
FBY 724	Ford R1014	Duple Dominant II	C45F	8/78	by 8/86	Joseph Borg, Mellieha
FBY 725	AEC Mercury GM4RH	Barbara	B40F	unknown	9/67	Nazzareno Abela, Zejtun
FBY 726	AEC Reliance MU3RV	Aquilina (1971)	B45F	1954	6/90	Victor Meli, Mosta
FBY 727	Volvo B6BLE	Scarnif	N45F	5/02	5/02	Saviour Vella, Zejtun
FBY 728	Bedford SB	Debono	B45F	1958	1958	Carmel Cutajar, Pieta
FBY 729	Bedford YLQ	Duple Dominant II	C45F	4/77	6/86	Stephen Cilia, Gharghur
FBY 730	AEC Mercury GM4RAE	Barbara	B45F	unknown	by 9/85	Auxilio Caruana, Mosta
FBY 731	Ford ET7	Aquilina	B36F	4/53	4/53	Horace Vella, Qormi
FBY 732	*This registration is currently not in use.*					Anthony Buttigieg, Marsaskala
FBY 733	Maltese Docks/AEC MP	Brincat	DP36F	1992	1992	Rosaria Falzon, Fgura
FBY 734	Bedford SB3	Debono	B40F	1958	by 8/74	Sonia Falzon, Qrendi
FBY 735	Bedford YRQ	Duple Dominant I	B45F	9/73	1/85	Giuseppa Abela, Rabat

FBY 721, Y-0721, Y-1422, A-3286, 3286 — Of unknown origin
FBY 722, Y-0722, PEX 738W — Norfolk County Council
FBY 723, Y-0723, Y-1424, A-3288, JGF 803K — London Transport, SMS 803
FBY 724, Y-0724, LHO 418T — Marchwood, Totton
FBY 725, Y-0725, Y-1426, A-3290, 3290 — Of unknown origin
FBY 726, Y-0726, Y-0876, Y-1576, A-764, 764, TUA 17 — Unscheduled bus, Malta
FBY 727 — New
FBY 728, Y-0728, Y-1429, A-3293, 3293 — New (*This vehicle was rebuilt between June '89 and May '92*)
FBY 729, Y-0729, RAW 27R — Daniel, Cardigan
FBY 730, Y-0730, Y-1431, A-3297, 602 — Route bus, Malta
FBY 731, Y-0731, Y-1432, A-3298, 3298 — New
FBY 732
FBY 733, Y-0733 — New
FBY 734, Y-0734, Y-1435, A-3302, 3302 — Of unknown origin
FBY 735, Y-0735, OOT 267M — Pulfrey, Great Gonerby

FBY 745 is seen at Sliema Ferry, the terminus of route 645 to Cirkewwa, on 5th August 2001.

FBY 736	Bedford SB	Barbara (1973)	B39F	unknown	3/73	Grace Caruana, Zabbar	
FBY 737	Bedford YRQ	Duple Dominant I	DP45F	6/75	3/86	Joseph Vella, Mellieha	
FBY 738	AEC Swift 4MP2R	Marshall	B46F	1/70	5/81	Joseph Refalo, Santa Venera	
FBY 739	Maltese Docks f/c	Daina	B41F	unknown	3/83	Joseph Azzopardi, Attard	
FBY 740	Dodge f/c	Aquilina	B40F	5/54	5/54	Renard Demanuele, Zabbar	
FBY 741	AEC Mercury GMR4H	Barbara	B40F	unknown	12/64	Saviour Caruana, Qormi	
FBY 742	Dennis Dart SLF	East Lancs	N45F	3/97	3/97	Leone Grech, Mosta	
FBY 743	Maltese Docks f/c	Sammut	B40F	unknown	3/75	Jimmy Sammut, San Pawl il-Bahar	
FBY 744	AEC Swift 4MP2R1	Park Royal	B46F	10/70	5/81	Antoine Sant, Mellieha	
FBY 745	Albion f/c	Aquilina	B40F	unknown	12/79	Anthony Zarb, Dingli	
FBY 746	Bedford YRQ	Duple Dominant I	DP45F	5/73	by 11/84	Alfred Mercieca, Marsa	
FBY 747	Bedford YRQ	Plaxton Panorama Elite II	B45F	2/71	by 3/85	Nazzareno Fenech, Zebbug	
FBY 748	AEC Reliance 4MU3RA	Brincat	B45F	1962	by 1/89	Charles Cortis, Naxxar	
FBY 749	AEC Mercury 2GM4RA	Debono (1966)	B40F	1959	by 2/68	Thomas Joseph Psaila, Luqa	
FBY 750	Dodge KR900	Aquilina (1972)	B43F	1966	by 7/87	Joseph Gatt, Qormi	
FBY 751	Bedford YRQ	Duple Dominant I	DP45F	2/75	by 4/85	Richard Borg, Mosta	
FBY 752	Diamond T	Aquilina (1954)	B36F	11/50	3/54	Mario Mifsud, Mgarr	
FBY 753	Ford ET f/c	Barbara (1972)	B40F	c1962	3/72	Alphonse Abela, Ghaxaq	
FBY 754	Bedford YRQ	Duple Dominant I	C45F	1/75	by 1/85	Horace Vella, Qormi	
FBY 755	Bedford SBO	Vella	B40F	1954	by 8/74	Joseph Cassar, Kalkara	
FBY 756	AEC Swift 4MP2R1	Park Royal	B45F	10/70	4/81	David Borg, Mellieha	
FBY 757	Bedford YLQ	Duple Dominant I	C45F	2/77	by 5/92	Emanuel Farrugia, Zurrieq	
FBY 758	Bedford f/c	Aquilina (1960)	B40F	unknown	9/60	Philip Farrugia, Qormi	
FBY 759	Ford f/c	Casha	B40F	unknown	by 8/74	Anthony Micallef, Mosta	
FBY 760	Inter f/c	Sammut	B36F	1944	by 12/54	Sandro Abela, Zejtun	
FBY 761	*This registration is currently not in use.*					Anton Gatt, Zejtun	
FBY 762	Bedford YRQ	Plaxton Panorama Elite III Exp	C45F	3/76	by 11/84	Andrew Abela, Zejtun	
FBY 763	AEC Swift 4MP2R	Marshall	B46F	2/70	by 5/81	Adrian Caruana, Zabbar	
FBY 764	Bedford RL	Aquilina (1963)	B40F	1956	11/63	Joseph Vella, Mgarr	
FBY 765	*This registration is currently not in use.*					Abela Carmelo, Zejtun	

FBY 742 is to be frequently seen on lay-over near the Bugibba Holiday Complex in early evening – just as it was on 30th July 2001.

FBY 736, Y-0736, Y-1437, A-3307, 3307	Ministry of Defence
FBY 737, Y-0737, HGM 822N	Reliance, Newbury, 147
FBY 738, Y-0738, Y-1439, A-3309, AML 9H	London Transport, SM9
FBY 739, Y-0739, Y-0903, Y-1603, A-434, 434	Unscheduled bus, Malta
FBY 740, Y-0740, Y-1441, A-3311, 3311	New
FBY 741, Y-0741, Y-1442, A-3312, 3312	Of unknown origin
FBY 742	New
FBY 743, Y-0743, Y-1444, A-3314, 3314, 3846	Unscheduled bus, Malta
FBY 744, Y-0744, Y-1445, A-3315, EGN 258J	London Transport, SMS 258
FBY 745, Y-0745, Y-1446, A-3316	Of unknown origin
FBY 746, Y-0746, NMB 279L	Romani, Bridgwater
FBY 747, Y-0747, ABW 183J	Calloway, Rowley Regis
FBY 748, Y-0748, Y-0906, Y-1606, A-5574, 5574, 336 VLG	Unscheduled bus, Malta
FBY 749, Y-0749, Y-1450, A-3320, 3320	Of unknown origin
FBY 750, Y-0750, Y-0904, Y-1604, A-5301, 5301	Unscheduled bus, Malta
FBY 751, Y-0751, Y-1452, GUX 401N	Trefaldwyn, Montgomery
FBY 752, Y-0752, Y-1453, A-3324, 3324, 2350	Route bus, Malta
FBY 753, Y-0753, Y-1454, A-3325, 3325, 2538	Route bus, Malta
FBY 754, Y-0754, Y-1455, GUX 400N	Wigston Coach Hire
FBY 755, Y-0755, Y-1456, A-3329, 3329	Of unknown origin
FBY 756, Y-0756, Y-1457, A-3330, EGN 275J	London Transport, SMS 275
FBY 757, Y-0757, YAA 261R	Marchwood, Totton
FBY 758, Y-0758, Y-1459, A-3332, 3332	Ministry of Defence crane
FBY 759, Y-0759, Y-1460, A-3335, 3335, 1767	Route bus, Malta
FBY 760, Y-0760, Y-1461, A-3336, 3336	English fire engine
FBY 761	
FBY 762, Y-0762, Y-1463, LRG 65P	Williams, Brecon
FBY 763, Y-0763, Y-1464, A-3339, AML 34H	London Transport, SMS 34
FBY 764, Y-0764, Y-1465, A-3340, 3340	Ministry of Defence lorry
FBY 765	

FBY 766 is seen operating route 154, the unique Naxxar Town Council service, as it passes through Maghtab on 3rd August 2001.

FBY 766	Bedford f/c	Barbara	B40F	unknown	2/68	Charles Vella, Mosta
FBY 767	AEC Reliance MU3RV	Debono (1970)	DP45F	1955	by 7/87	John Camilleri, Naxxar
FBY 768	Dennis Falcon H SDA 413	East Lancs	DP43F	2/85	1/02	Albert Refalo, Attard
FBY 769	AEC Mercury	Farrugia	B40F	unknown	by 2/68	Sebastian Ciappara, Qormi
FBY 770	Leyland TS or TD	Barbara (1958)	B40F	unknown	7/58	Anthony Mifsud, Zurrieq
FBY 771	AEC Regal 0662	Barbara	B40F	1939	3/59	Carmelo Carobott, Zetjun
FBY 772	*This registration is currently not in use.*					Victor Meli, Mosta
FBY 773	AEC Swift 4MP2R	Marshall	B46F	5/70	9/80	Joseph Borg, Zabbar
FBY 774	AEC Mercury 2GM4RA	Aquilina (1965)	B40F	1958	10/65	Sebastian Mifsud, Mellieha
FBY 775	Dodge f/c	Zammit	B40F	unknown	by 9/73	Jesmond Azzopardi, Attard
FBY 776	AEC Swift 4MP2R1	Park Royal	B46F	10/70	by 12/82	Wilfred Cardona, Marsa
FBY 777	AEC Mercury GMR4H	Farrugia (1965)	B40F	1958	11/65	Charles Vella, Mosta
FBY 778	Bedford SB	Brincat (1873)	B40F	unknown	by 10/88	Martin Borg, Mellieha
FBY 779	AEC Swift 4MP2R1	Park Royal	B46F	11/70	5/81	Patrick Cauchi, Mellieha
FBY 780	Bedford YRQ	Duple Dominant I Express	C45F	8/74	by 4/85	Rosaria Falzon, Fgura

FBY 766, Y-0766, Y-1467, A-3342, 3342	Of unknown origin
FBY 767, Y-0767, Y-0871, Y-1571, A-2573, 2573, OWT 940	Unscheduled bus, Malta
FBY 768, B51 XFV	Pilkington, Accrington (originally Hyndburn 51)
FBY 769, Y-0769, Y-1470, A-3346, 3346	Of unknown origin
FBY 770, Y-0770, Y-1471, A-3347, 3347	Of unknown origin
FBY 771, Y-0771, Y-1472, A-3348, 3348, CU 4265	Northern General, 925
FBY 772	
FBY 773, Y-0773, Y-1474, A-3350, AML 50H	London Transport, SMS 50
FBY 774, Y-0774, Y-1475, A-3351, 3351	Of unknown origin
FBY 775, Y-0775, Y-1476, A-3352, 3352	Of unknown origin
FBY 776, Y-0776, Y-1477, EGN 238J	London Transport, SMS 238
FBY 777, Y-0777, Y-1478, A-3354, 3354	Of unknown origin
FBY 778, Y-0778, Y-0923, Y-1623, A-1788, 1788	Unscheduled bus, Malta
FBY 779, Y-0779, Y-1480, A-3356, EGN 280J	London Transport, SMS 280
FBY 780, Y-0780, OHB 470N	Williams, Brecon

FBY 782 is the first of the new breed of low-floor vehicles delivered to Malta. It is seen, still unregistered, very near to its home premises of Cancu Supreme at Zejtun on 27th July 2001.

FBY 781	Bedford QL	Barbara (1951)	B36F	unknown	12/51	Etienne Falzon, Qormi
FBY 782	King Long XMQ6113	King Long	N45F	7/01	7/01	Nazzareno Abela, Zejtun
FBY 783	*This registration is currently not in use.*					Felix Fenech, Mosta
FBY 784	unknown f/c	Debono	B40F	unknown	by 8/74	Carmel Caruana, Zebbug
FBY 785	Leyland Tiger Cub PSUC1/13	East Lancs	B46F	1/67	by 8/81	Charles Vella, Mosta
FBY 786	Bedford YLQ	Duple Dominant II	C45F	unknown	by 4/88	Raymond Buttigieg, Zabbar
FBY 787	Leyland Tiger Cub PSUC1/13	Scarnif	B45F	1967	by 8/81	Jason Borg, Zebbug
FBY 788	Maltese Docks f/c	Schembri	B40F	by 4/73	by 4/73	Francis Bugeja, Cospicua
FBY 789	*This registration is currently not in use.*					Mario Sultana, Cospicua
FBY 790	Bedford YRQ	Plaxton Panorama Elite III	B45F	2/76	7/85	Carmel k/a Charles Galea, Sliema
FBY 791	Maltese Docks/Dodge 310	Aquilina (1975)	DP40F	unknown	by 4/94	Leone Grech, Mosta
FBY 792	Maltese Docks	Tonna	B40F	unknown	by 8/74	Mario Sultana, Bormla
FBY 793	Bedford YRQ	Duple Dominant I	C45F	7/73	by 3/87	Carmelo Abela, Rabat
FBY 794	Mercedes Benz f/c	Sammut	B36F	1956	1956	Angelo Sciberras, Qrendi
FBY 795	*This registration is currently not in use.*					Joseph Cutajar, Mqabba

FBY 781, Y-0781, Y-1482, A-3359, 3359   Of unknown origin
FBY 782   New
FBY 783
FBY 784, Y-0784, Y-1485, A-3495, 3495, 6512   Gozo post bus
FBY 785, Y-0785, Y-1486, A-3548, FCB 12D   Blackburn, 12
FBY 786, Y-0786, SCD 899R   Plumpton Coaches
FBY 787, Y-0787, Y-1488, A-3673, GBV 18E   Blackburn, 18 (*This vehicle was rebuilt by Scarnif in 2000/01 and received a Scarnif "Broadway" body.*)
FBY 788, Y-0788, Y-1489, A-3674, 3674   New
FBY 789
FBY 790, Y-0790, NFW 574P   Bird, North Hykeham
FBY 791, Y-0791, Y-0852, Y-1552, A-3440, 3440   Unscheduled bus, Malta
FBY 792, Y-0792, Y-1493, A-4757, 4757   Of unknown origin
FBY 793, Y-0793, MUE 648L   Woodcock, Buxton
FBY 794, Y-0794, Y-1495, A-4759 , 4759   New
FBY 795

FBY 805, the island's sole Optare Excel, passes through Gudja on its return journey from Luqa Airport to Valletta on 27th March 2002. Note that, despite the provision of a destination box and route box, neither is used; the route number is on the board in the windscreen, instead.

FBY 796	Bedford YRQ	Plaxton Panorama Elite III	C45F	9/74	by 11/84	Rennie Bonnici, Birzebuggia
FBY 797	AEC Swift 4MP2R1	Marshall	B46F	1/71	9/80	Emmanuel Psaila, Zurrieq
FBY 798	AEC Reliance 2MU4RA	Barbara	B40F	3/64	3/64	Antoinette Abela, Zejtun
FBY 799	AEC Regal 0662	Schembri	B40F	1938	by 12/79	Carlo Bonavia, Fgura
FBY 800	Bedford f/c	Farrugia (1968)	B40F	unknown	by 2/55	Mark Tonna, Marsa
FBY 801	Leyland Titan TD5c	Brincat	B36F	1937	by 4/94	Michael Mifsud, Qormi
FBY 802	*This registration is currently not in use.*					Joseph Borg, Zabbar
FBY 803	Bedford SB	Barbara (1973)	B39F	unknown	3/73	George Aquilina, Gzira
FBY 804	Bedford SB	Debono	B40F	unknown	by 10/88	Joseph Buhagiar, Zebbug
FBY 805	Optare Excel L1060	Optare	N45F	2/97	2/97	Annunziata Abela, Zejtun
FBY 806	Maltese Docks f/c	Zammit	B40F	unknown	1979	Victor Muscat, Mosta
FBY 807	Bedford YRQ	Marshall	B46F	7/75	by 4/89	Francis Abela, Zejtun
U/R	Chongqing	Chongqing	N45F	9/01	9/01	Demonstrator
U/R	Dennis Dart SLF	Neobus	N45F	8/02	8/02	Demonstrator

FBY 796, Y-0796, Y-1497, SJR 428N — Dobson, Whickham
FBY 797, Y-0797, Y-1498, A-5293, EGN 194J — London Transport, SMS 194
FBY 798, Y-0798, Y-1499, A-5294, 5294 — New
FBY 799, Y-0799, Y-1500, A-1548, 571, AHJ 404 — Route bus, Malta (originally Westcliff-on-Sea Motor Services)
(This vehicle received its Schembri body during 1964)

FBY 800, Y-0800, Y-1501, A-5568, 5568 — Of unknown origin
FBY 801, Y-0801, Y-0909, Y-1609, A-0732, 0732, WH 9202 — Unscheduled bus, Malta (originally Bolton Transport)
FBY 802
FBY 803, Y-0803, Y-1504, A-5576, 5576 — Of unknown origin
FBY 804, Y-0804, Y-0862, Y-1562, A-2482, 2482 — Unscheduled bus, Malta
FBY 805, Y-0805 — New
FBY 806, Y-0806, Y-1507, 2507 — Of unknown origin
FBY 807, Y-0807, HGM 616N — Atomic Weapons Research Establishment, Aldermaston

THE HISTORY OF BUSES ON GOZO

The early history of public transport on the island of Gozo was restricted to the use of the traditional horse-drawn carriages, called a *Karrozzin*. As the islands were British colonies, it was logical that English-sourced vehicles eventually appeared on Gozo, with some originating from the Army after 1945. These military vehicles were converted into buses. Other buses of American origin were brought to Gozo, too.

During the Second World War, services continued to function as circumstances allowed, but they were reduced or restricted according to the availability of fuel, and some routes were cancelled. A well-known story, still often told, recalls how driver Joseph Caruana had left his bus in Sabina Square in Victoria when trying to run away from a bomb dropped near his bus. He was wounded, but the bus remained intact.

In 1945 Joseph, nicknamed "Kelies", because he had owned a horse-drawn carriage before the war, bought a Federal, numbered 1250. The bus had 24 seats, and a rear entrance. When on duty, Joseph wore a cap and if he was caught without it he was heavily fined. Even travelling without a conductor brought fines, and the vehicle could also be "garaged" for up to a maximum of eight days. Joseph's bus was one of fourteen on the island. During the early years after WW2, these buses were each painted a different colour to indicate the route and village served. The bus based at Victoria served the harbour at Mgarr, Marsalforn on the north coast, Ta Pinu and Xlendi. It boasted a grey, white and red livery. The Nadur bus was green, Xaghra red, with the owners choosing the colour schemes for themselves. The bus allocated to one route was prohibited from operating on any other.

FBY 045, an AEC Reliance with Ciantar body, waits for its group of day-visitors to the island to return after their visit to Victoria, the island's capital, on Maundy Thursday, April 12th 2001.

The fourteen buses were reduced to twelve after the Government intervened in the early 1950s, stating that there two too many buses on the island. Lots were cast to decide whose vehicles would be taken off the road and sold to Maltese owners. Joseph had to sell one of his buses, as did the Nadur driver.

During the 1950s there were no foreign tourists coming to Gozo, merely local migration between the villages. Bus travel was principal form of transport for the Gozitans, as private cars were virtually unknown. A bus owner/driver had to endure long working-hours, beginning at 05:00 and often working until 23:00, but he was able to make a good living. Fares varied from route to route, according to the distance from Victoria of the village served. When Joseph's son, Emanuel, began working as a conductor on his father's bus, at the age of ten, he was paid at the rate of one pound ten shillings per week (£1 50p).

In 1959 the bus owners formed an Association on the island. From then onwards the routes were operated on a roster basis. The various colour schemes for the buses were discontinued and the colour scheme of the Victoria bus (grey, with a white roof, and one red band at waist level) was chosen for the island's whole fleet, a colour scheme which continues to this day. Local private work on the island was based on free enterprise.

In the early 1960s a Sunday service from Xaghra to Victoria was introduced, starting at 16:00 and finishing at 21:00, to cater for local residents wishing to go to the cinema. This service remained unique to Xaghra for most of the decade, but during the 1970s most of the other villages boasted similar services. By the early 1980s these services had been withdrawn, however, the passage of time having been marked by the increased number of private cars on the island, owned especially by the younger generation.

Bus services on Gozo were not centralised on the present-day bus-station in Victoria until 1965. Until then individual routes boasted their own termini around the town. The terminus for the route to Mgarr was Independence Square; to Xaghra from near the Police Station; to Nadur, Xewkija, Qala and Marsalforn from Main Gate Street; to Xlendi from St Augustin Square; to Sannat from St Francis Square and to Gharb, San Lawrenz, Ghasri and Zebbug from Sabina Square. When the new bus station in Triq Putirjal was opened, the bus drivers soon went on strike, as their vehicles would not easily start on the upward hill towards St Francis Square.

The number of buses on the island gradually increased over the years. The original Gozo buses included a Federal, an Inter, a Reo and a Ford ET7 forward-control bus, each with a body by a Maltese builder, such as Borg, Casha or Debono. During the 1960s the number rose to 18 when a number of Bedford chassis with Leyland engines were bought new and were bodied, just as their sister vehicles on Malta, by Aquilina. A further ten buses arrived in 1974, some of which were buses transferred from Malta. During the mid-1980s vehicles imported from Britain appeared on the island. Two Bristol LHs preceded a number of Dominants, one Ford Plaxton and a Hino which were imported – either from Britain or from Malta — after the Government relaxed the laws limiting the size of vehicles. So, buses of 10 metres in length were permitted on the island's roads. The names of the lucky drivers receiving these vehicles were drawn by lot. Five years later another three vehicles were introduced, after a computer selection of the three new owners. This brought the total of buses on the island to 39. In 1996 the Government gave every driver permission to buy one new vehicle for each one he already owned to cater for the increase of tourism on the island.

Representative of the demonstrator vehicles which are now to be found on Gozo is FBY 003, the sole Iveco vehicle on the islands — which is seen at Xlendi at lunchtime on Maundy Thursday, 12th April 2001.

The present-day total of 78 buses and coaches still includes many of the vehicles involved in the development of the island's bus fleet outlined in the preceding paragraph. The doubling of the fleet brought a large number of coaches on Optimal chassis with bodies built on Malta by Scarnif. An array of distinctive demonstrator buses and coaches appeared too, on British, German or French chassis with bodies built by a wide choice of foreign builders, from Italy and Portugal, for instance.

The original buses on Gozo had seating for 32, 34 or 36 passengers. The present-day fleet consists principally of vehicles with 36, 45 or (for the coaches) 53 seats. Up to twelve standing passengers are allowed on route buses, with none on the coaches.

Registrations of the buses on Gozo have always been based on the series current in Malta. The original number-only sequence was superseded in 1979 by A-prefix registrations. Then the Y-prefix covered the period when there were the 39 buses on the island, with the buses being numbered from Y-0808 to Y-0846. The 1996/97 adoption of the FBY series on Gozo coincided with the arrival of the demonstrators and Paramount-bodied Bedford coaches on the island, the vehicles being registered FBY 001 to FBY 079, with 069 omitted.

There are eight buses operating the island's routes each day, with one (or two) vehicles being allocated to one specific route, or a series of interworked routes throughout the day.

Despatchers employed by the Transport Authority oversee arrivals and departures from the Bus Station. Private hire work is allocated on a roster basis by the GBOA, the Gozo Bus Owners' Association. Fares are 15c for each journey; with the popular destinations for holidaymakers of Ramla Bay and Dwejra (for the Inland Sea and Azure Window) costing 25c each way. Fares are imposed and regulated by the Government and cannot be altered without its authority.

Services to the villages run at a loss nowadays. But there is still a reasonable provision to all the principal villages on the island, with special journeys for school-children during the term-time to and from school in Victoria, and also for workers at the Industrial Estate, with an afternoon exodus on all routes at 16:00 Monday to Friday. During the summer months Marsalforn and Xlendi, in particular, have services every 45 or 60 minutes throughout the day. The timings to Marsalforn in summer 2002, for instance, totalled 24 a day, with extensions along the promenade to Qbajjar every two hours. The small villages of Santa Lucija and Kercem, on the other hand, have three early morning timings and then nothing else until the 16:00 works service. Unique amongst the Gozo routes this route does not start from the Bus Station, but from Sabina Square. Services from Victoria to the ferry at Mgarr leave thirty minutes before the ferry's departure throughout the day.

With Gozo being so small and Victoria being situated in the centre of the island, journey times on most routes are very short. The timetables at the main bus-station advise passengers that the return journey from the outer terminus will usually be about ten minutes after the departure time from Victoria. Exceptions to this are to be found on the almost hour-long route 91 to Gharb, Dwejra and Zebbug, or route 42 to Nadur and Ramla Bay. But even these normal timetabled services can take on an aspect all their own, as the author found in summer 2001. After travelling to Nadur and Ramla Bay on Saturday August 4th, he was then taken to Xewkija, Munxar, Sannat, Kercem, and then via the back streets of Victoria to Ta' Pinu Church with a party of pensioners all chanting Catholic responses throughout their journey for three quarters of an hour, with the author's lasting a few minutes short of two hours!

Emanuel Caruana is now the longest serving owner-driver on the island, having begun driving for his father when seventeen years old, in 1967. He can laugh now about his early days, but when he first became a driver, regular passengers queried his ability and qualification to do so at such a tender age. Another owner-driver, Anthony Caruana, has been driving for 26 years. Owners are proud of their vehicles which are kept in immaculate condition.

Each of the 78 buses is unique, not necessarily because of its vehicle type, body or chassis, but because of the application of the red band in its colour scheme, or its individual wording on windscreen or bodywork. Emanuel Cutajar's Bedford (FBY 032) proclaims *SPEEDWAY GARAGE* on its front windscreen; similarly, Joe Scerri's Bedford (FBY 061) proudly and incongruously shows *GEORGE EDWARDS AND SON* on the front windscreen and *Coachmen since 1923* at the rear, thus still indicating the former owner of the coach near Wrexham, north Wales; Optimal/Scarnif FBY 078 has *SECRETS* to reveal, whilst a similar vehicle FBY 075 shows *LEPEIRKS Coaches,* which is merely the nickname of the owner, Skriepel, spelt backwards. Amongst the older vehicles the Reo (FBY 042) shows its nickname *DOLLY,* and Bedford SB (FBY 038) shows *CLOUDS.* Many drivers are employed, some part-time, by the owners nowadays. As on Malta, many of the vehicles are garaged overnight at the homes of their owners in villages throughout the island. Consequently, the daily timetable of the final departure from Victoria of some of the routes bears the unusual proviso "This service does not return to Victoria".

Awaiting passengers at Mgarr, again on Maundy Thursday 2001, is the one vehicle on Gozo with something of an unknown heritage. FBY 007 has a Leyland chassis, but its age and bodywork are unknown.

FBY 058, a Dennis Javelin with Duple bodywork, pauses in Sabina Square, Victoria, as a large group of Italian tourists alight on their way to an English language course in the capital, on 31st July 2001.

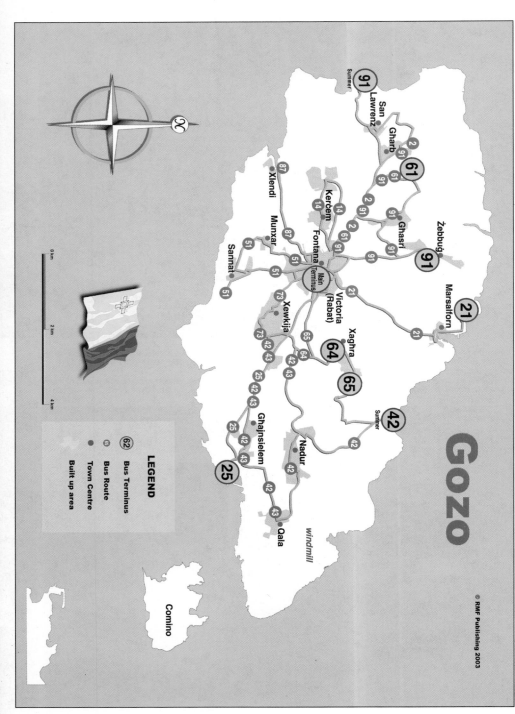

VEHICLES ON GOZO

FBY 001	Bedford YNV Venturer	Caetano Algarve N-NDH	C53F	3/88	5/87	Carmelo Cauchi, Xewkija
FBY 002	MAN 11.192	Dorteller	B45F	by 1/93	6/97	Jason Farrugia, Victoria
FBY 003	Iveco 380	Cacciamali	B45D	by 12/96	6/97	Jason Farrugia, Victoria
FBY 004	Dennis Javelin 11SDL1905	Plaxton Paramount 3200 III	C53F	7/88	6/97	Anthony Debono, Nadur
FBY 005	Mercedes Benz 1310/50	Castrosua	B45F	by 1/91	6/97	Jason Farrugia, Victoria
FBY 006	ERF E6.18BC2	Marshall	B45F	4/95	6/97	Phillip Bonnici, Sannat
FBY 007	Leyland f/c	unknown	B45F	unknown	6/97	John Attard, Xaghra
FBY 008	Dennis Javelin 11SDA1906	Plaxton Paramount 3200 III	C53F	8/89	8/97	Emanuel Cutajar, Victoria
FBY 009	Sanos S315-21	Sanos Carisma	C53F	5/90	6/97	Joseph Portelli, Gharb
FBY 010	Dennis Javelin 11SDL1905	Plaxton Paramount 3200 III	C53F	9/87	8/97	George Tabone, Fontana
FBY 011	Bedford YNT	Plaxton Paramount 3200 III	C53F	3/87	8/97	Emanuel Mintoff, Ghasri
FBY 012	Optimal	Scarnif	C53F	9/97	9/97	Phillip Bonnici, Sannat
FBY 013	Dennis Javelin 11SDL1905	Plaxton Paramount 3200 III	C53F	10/88	8/97	Teddy Cassar, Victoria
FBY 014	Dennis Javelin 12SDA1908	Plaxton Paramount 3200 III	C53F	3/88	by 3/98	Emanuel Custo, Gharb

FBY 001, 6541 FN, E348 TPW	Caroline Seagull, Great Yarmouth
FBY 002	Maltese demonstrator
FBY 003	Maltese demonstrator
FBY 004, E538 PRU	Lewis, Llanrhystyd
FBY 005	Maltese demonstrator
FBY 006	Maltese demonstrator
FBY 007	Route bus, Malta (*The original identity of this vehicle has not been verified*)
FBY 008, G778 APK	Bicknell, Godalming
FBY 009, G895 VNA	R. & N. Lyles, Batley
FBY 010, E839 EUT	Bicknell, Godalming
FBY 011, HIL2385, D390 BNR	Hearn, Harrow Weald
FBY 012	New
FBY 013, F900 RFH	Stevens, Bristol
FBY 014, E514 WAH, WOA 521, E511 JWP	Sanders, Holt

FBY 028 is one of the two Hino buses on Gozo. It is seen departing with a party of day-trippers from the ferry terminal at Mgarr at about 10:00 on 26th March 2002.

FBY 015	Bedford SB	Zammit	B36F	1962	by 8/74	Michael Caruana, Xaghra
FBY 016	Bedford YRQ	Plaxton Panorama Elite III	C45F	9/74	3/90	Michael Farrugia, Victoria
FBY 017	Bedford YNT	Plaxton Paramount 3200 I	C53F	3/85	6/93	Emanuel Mintoff, Ghasri
FBY 018	Bedford YLQ	Duple Dominant II	C45F	3/78	7/88	Phillip Bonnici, Sannat
FBY 019	Bedford SB	Aquilina	B36F	unknown	by 12/72	Phillip Bonnici, Sannat
FBY 020	AEC Reliance 6U3ZR	Duple Dominant II	C53F	5/79	by 10/91	Phillip Bonnici, Sannat
FBY 021	Ford ET7 f/c	Borg	B40F	4/53	4/53	Phillip Bonnici, Sannat
FBY 022	Albion f/c	Aquilina	B36F	7/68	7/68	Mariano Farugia, Xewkija
FBY 023	Bedford YRQ	Duple Dominant I	C45F	3/75	12/87	Raymond Pace, Kercem
FBY 024	Leyland Leopard PSU3/1R	Plaxton Supreme II (1977)	C53F	5/62	by 4/91	Emanuel Tabone, Munxar
FBY 025	Bedford SB8	Aquilina	B36F	2/62	2/62	Saviour Buttigieg, Qala
FBY 026	Bedford SB8	Aquilina	B36F	5/63	5/63	John Attard, Xaghra
FBY 027	Inter K f/c	Casha	B36F	1942	by 9/74	George Tabone, Fontana
FBY 028	Hino BT51	Debono	DP36F	1977	by 7/88	Teddy Cassar, Victoria
FBY 029	Bedford YLQ	Duple Dominant II	C45F	9/79	7/88	John Portelli, Gharb
FBY 030	Bedford YRQ	Duple Dominant I	C45F	9/75	by 4/86	Ludovico Azzopardi, Zebbug
FBY 031	Bedford YMT	Duple Dominant I	C53F	6/76	by 3/86	Joseph Grima, Qala

FBY 015, Y-0827, Y-1528, A-3095, 3095	Route bus, Malta
FBY 016, Y-0821, Y-0466, UUP 2N	Route bus, Malta
FBY 017, Y-0845, B493 BJO, 499 BHU, B730 YNM	Majestic, Shareshill
FBY 018, Y-0841, AGG 934S	Chapman, Airdrie
FBY 019, Y-0818, Y-1519, A-2483, 2483	Of unknown origin
FBY 020, Y-0820, BHL 472T	Ash, Woodburn Moor
FBY 021, Y-0824, Y-1525, A-3062, 3062	New
FBY 022, Y-0830. Y-1531, A-3184, 3184	New
FBY 023, Y-0839, HSG 724N	Bland, Stamford
FBY 024, Y-0809, Y-0897, OBN 534R, 6781 DD	Unscheduled bus, Malta *(rebodied during 1977)*
FBY 025, Y-0832, Y-1535, C-1503, 31503	New
FBY 026, Y-0825, Y-1526, A-3065, 3065	New
FBY 027, Y-0810, Y-1511, A-1126, 1126	Route bus, Malta
FBY 028, Y-0840, Y-0888, Y-1588, A-2362, 2362	Unscheduled bus, Malta
FBY 029, Y-0842, YRG 702V	Glyn Evans, Manmoel
FBY 030, Y-0813, KPC 213P	Reliance, Newbury, 157
FBY 031, Y-0831, LTF 224P	Reliance, Newbury, 149

FBY 038 is parked outside its owner's home in Victoria, Gozo's capital, on 30th July 1999.

FBY 032	Bedford YNT	Plaxton Paramount 3200 II	C53F	3/86	7/93	Emanuel Cutajar, Victoria
FBY 033	Bedford YRQ	Duple Dominant I	C45F	2/76	5/88	Joe Scerri, Xaghra
FBY 034	Bedford YMT	Duple Dominant II	C53F	5/77	by 6/00	Mary Caruana, Victoria
FBY 035	Bristol LH6L	Eastern Coach Works	B45F	12/74	by 9/85	Anthony Caruana, Victoria
FBY 036	Ford R1014	Plaxton Supreme IV Express	C45F	4/81	5/88	Bernadette Custo, Gharb
FBY 037	Leyland Royal Tiger PSU1/15	Schembri (1973)	B36C	1953	6/73	Anthony Debono, Nadur
FBY 038	Bedford SB	Debono	B36F	2/35	by 12/69	Jason Farrugia, Victoria
FBY 039	Bedford YNT	Plaxton Paramount 3200	C53F	4/84	7/93	Albert Farrugia, Victoria
FBY 040	Bedford f/c	Aquilina	B36F	4/56	11/56	Jason Farrugia, Victoria
FBY 041	Bedford YLQ	Duple Dominant II	C45F	2/79	7/88	Jason Farrugia, Victoria
FBY 042	Reo f/c	Zammit	B36F	10/62	by 3/74	Jason Farrugia, Victoria
FBY 043	Dodge T110	Aquilina	B36F	5/35	4/54	Jason Farrugia, Victoria
FBY 044	Bedford SB8	Aquilina	B36F	5/62	5/62	Jason Farrugia, Victoria
FBY 045	AEC Reliance 2MU3RA	Ciantar	C45F	1960	3/86	Carmelo Cauchi, Xewkija
FBY 046	Bedford YNT	Plaxton Paramount 3200 III	C53F	8/87	8/97	Emanuel Caruana, Victoria
FBY 047	Bedford YNT	Plaxton Paramount 3200 III	C53F	8/87	8/97	Raymond Pace, Kercem
FBY 048	Bristol LH6L	Plaxton Supreme II	C45F	1/78	4/86	Rita Farrugia, Xewkija

FBY 032, Y-0846, D354 CFR, BIB 7667, C212 DEC	Bibby, Ingleton
FBY 033, Y-0838, MRB 686P	Clarke, Newthorpe
FBY 034, LCY 860, Y-0860, SBC 57R	Unscheduled bus, Malta
FBY 035, Y-0811, Y-1512, GLJ 482N	Hants and Dorset, 3550
FBY 036, Y-0837, MJX 791W	Stopps, Uxbridge
FBY 037, Y-0815, Y-1516, A-2070, 2070, FCK 402	Wimpey, London W6
FBY 038, Y-0817, Y-1518, A-2377, 2377	Ministry of Defence
FBY 039, Y-0844, JPY 505, A468 MRW, 9258 VC, A838 PPP	Whittle, Kidderminster
FBY 040, Y-0828, Y-1529, A-3126, 3126	Lorry
FBY 041, Y-0843, JTU 227T	Bostock, Congleton, 26
FBY 042, Y-0816, Y-1517, A-2296, 2296	Route bus, Malta
FBY 043, Y-0822, Y-1523, A-2844, 2844	Route bus, Malta
FBY 044, Y-0834, Y-1533, C-1506, 31506	New
FBY 045, Y-0826, Y-0880, Y-1580, A-3117, 3117, YXD 11	Unscheduled bus, Malta
FBY 046, SJI 7046, E848 KCF, OVK 902, E829 EUT	Venture, Harrow
FBY 047, HIL 3478, D865 ATF	Hill, Congleton
FBY 048, Y-0829, WJN 22S	Stowell, Fearnhead

FBY 057 arrives in the broad village-square dominated by the imposing church at Gharb on 30th July 1999, on the 16:00 service of route 91. This particular timing, along with one on each of the other daily routes on the island, leaves from the Industrial Estate enabling the workers to travel home after their day's shift.

FBY 049	Bedford YNT	Plaxton Supreme V	C53F	10/81	12/93	John Portelli, Gharb
FBY 050	Bedford YLQ	Duple Dominant Express II	C45F	4/79	by 7/88	Michael Cini, Xaghra
FBY 051	Bedford SB8	Aquilina	B36F	2/62	2/62	Carmel Galea, Xaghra
FBY 052	Hino BT51	Debono	DP45F	by 12/76	by 12/76	John Caruana, Victoria
FBY 053	Bedford SB8	Aquilina	B36F	4/62	4/62	Carmel Cini, Xewkija
FBY 054	Bedford YMT	Plaxton Supreme III	C53F	6/76	3/86	Paul Borg, Victoria
FBY 055	Bedford YNT	Plaxton Paramount 3200 III	C53F	5/87	10/97	Anthony Caruana, Victoria
FBY 056	Dennis Javelin 11SDL1905	Plaxton Paramount 3200 III	C53F	1/89	9/97	Emanuel Tabone, Munxar
FBY 057	Maltese Docks f/c	Barbara	B36F	4/69	4/69	Jason Farrugia, Victoria
FBY 058	Dennis Javelin 11SDL1905	Duple 320 Express	C53F	4/88	by 11/97	Albert Farrugia, Victoria
FBY 059	Bedford YNV Venturer	Duple 320	C57F	3/88	9/97	Albert Farrugia, Victoria
FBY 060	Bedford YNT	Plaxton Paramount 3200 III	C53F	8/88	10/97	Carmel Galea, Xaghra
FBY 061	Bedford YNT	Plaxton Paramount 3200 III	C53F	8/87	9/97	Joe Scerri, Xaghra
FBY 062	Dennis Javelin 11SDL1921	Plaxton Paramount 3200 III	C53F	10/91	by 4/98	Ludovico Azzopardi, Zebbug
FBY 063	Sanos S315-21	Sanos Carisma	C53F	5/90	6/97	Carmel Cini, Xewkija
FBY 064	Dennis Javelin 10SDL2123	Duple Metsec	B45F	1993	by 5/98	Albert Farrugia, Victoria

FBY 049, Y-0814, Y-0889, VPR 864X	Unscheduled bus, Malta
FBY 050, Y-0836, OPT 471T	Tindall, Low Fell
FBY 051, Y-0835, 31504	New
FBY 052, Y-0823, Y-1524, A-3017, 3017	New
FBY 053, Y-0833, Y-1534, C-1505, 31505	New
FBY 054, Y-0812, PGT 527P	County, Brentwood
FBY 055, D614 GDU, 4828 VC, D677 FWK	Roy Brown, Builth Wells
FBY 056, F386 MUT	Brodyr James, Llangeitho
FBY 057, Y-0819, Y-1520, A-2522, 2522	New
FBY 058, GIL 8488, E38 SBO	Stone, Aldershot
FBY 059, E252 PEL	Richards Bros., Cardigan
FBY 060, KSU 363, F327 YTG	Brylaine, Boston
FBY 061, E370 ECJ	George Edwards & Son, Bwlchgwyn
FBY 062, J733 KBC	Warrington, Ilam
FBY 063, G894 VNA	R. & N. Lyles, Batley
FBY 064	Maltese demonstrator

On 4th August 2001, FBY 078 is seen parked at Dwejra Bay, the popular departure point for the Azure Window and Inland Sea. This destination is a regular venue for the day-trips organised by hotel chains for the Maltese holiday-makers, so many of the Gozitan coaches can be relied on to turn up here, especially on Mondays, Thursdays and Saturdays during the summer.

FBY 065	Bedford YNV Venturer	Caetano Algarve N-NDH	C53F	3/87	1/98	Michael Caruana, Xaghra
FBY 066	TAZ D3200	TAZ Dubrava	C53F	5/90	by 4/98	Paul Borg, Victoria
FBY 067	Bedford YNT	Plaxton Paramount 3200 III	C53F	5/87	3/98	Michael Farrugia, Victoria
FBY 068	Leyland Tiger TRCTL11/3RZ	Plaxton Paramount 3200 III	C53F	4/87	1/98	Michael Cini, Xaghra
FBY 069	*This registration has never been allocated.*					
FBY 070	Optimal	Scarnif	C53F	5/98	5/98	Phillip Bonnici, Sannat
FBY 071	Optimal	Scarnif	C53F	6/98	6/98	Joe Grima, Qala
FBY 072	Dennis Javelin 11SDA1906	Duple 320	C53F	4/89	by 11/98	Jason Farrugia, Victoria
FBY 073	Dennis Javelin 11SDA1905	Duple 320 Express	C53F	4/88	by 2/99	Jason Farrugia, Victoria
FBY 074	Optimal	Scarnif	C53F	8/98	8/98	Phillip Bonnici, Sannat
FBY 075	Optimal	Scarnif	C53F	8/98	8/98	Mariano & Rita Farrugia, Xewkija
FBY 076	Bedford YNV Venturer	Duple 320	C53F	4/87	by 2/99	John Caruana, Victoria
FBY 077	Optimal	Scarnif	C53F	11/98	11/98	John Portelli, Gharb
FBY 078	Optimal	Scarnif	C53F	c11/98	c11/98	Saviour Buttigieg, Qala
FBY 079	Optimal	Scarnif	C53F	by 5/98	by 5/99	Mariano Farrugia, Xewkija

FBY 065, D511 WNV	Ham, Flimwell
FBY 066, G579 WUT	Smith, High Wycombe
FBY 067, D854 XYJ	Trevann, Crawley
FBY 068, D64 MWO	Ham, Flimwell
FBY 070	New
FBY 071	New
FBY 072, 428 EJB, F906 UPR	Aron, Northolt
FBY 073, GIL 8487, E32 SBO	Quantum, Swadlincote
FBY 074	New
FBY 075	New
FBY 076, DIL 7916, D121 EFH	Hertfordshire Travel, Park Street
FBY 077	New
FBY 078	New
FBY 079	New

ROUTE 1 OR 2: VICTORIA TO GHARB/ST LAWRENZ
ROUTE 91: VICTORIA TO DWEJRA

This trio of routes covers the villages in the west of Gozo. Unusually vehicles do not always display a route number if working to Gharb, yet the departures to Dwejra always show 91.

On leaving Victoria and negotiating the sharp left-hand bend on the outskirts of the town, the bus soon passes the remains of an old aqueduct built in the 1840s by the British to carry water from Ghar Ilma to the capital. Then glimpses of Ta' Pinu Church along a road to the right are to be had. Gharb village is soon reached – its name means "west" – and it is the westernmost village on the island. The bus turns in the village square in front of the imposing parish church which was designed according to the plans of Francesco Borromini's Sant' Agnese in Agone at the Piazza Navona in Rome. The village is home to the island's Folklore Museum and to the workshops of Gozo Glass.

The bus then skirts the village and heads for San Lawrenz, where the Gozo Crafts Village is situated. Holidaymakers make full use of this route as, during the main tourist months, the bus will then travel down to Dwejra. Here boats are available to take tourists across the Inland Sea, through the natural tunnel in the cliffs to the Azure Window and Fungus Rock, the four natural wonders of the island. Four of the departures each day serve this spot.

The bus climbs back up to San Lawrenz, and then, depending on the timings, may serve San Pietru and Ghasri. Or else, it will head back in the direction of Victoria before turning left to pass by Ta' Pinu Church, the national shrine to the Blessed Virgin, built between 1920 and 1931. Opposite the church is a Way of the Cross up Ta' Ghammar Hill.

Ghasri is the smallest village on the island and is dominated by a lighthouse on Gordan Hill; its beam can be seen up to 50 kilometres away from its position 180 metres above sea level.

A rough minor road then brings the bus to the hill up to Zebbug, a village whose name means "olives" in Maltese. On a slope of one of the nearby hills there is a deposit of onyx. The village church is dedicated to Santa Marija. The local inhabitants are famed for their lace-making.

The bus turns, once again in the village square in front of the church, and returns the way it had come back down the hill, along the main roads back into Victoria. Unlike many of the other routes on the island which reach their outer destination in ten minutes or so from Victoria, this route, when serving Dwejra, can take up to an hour.

There are eight departures a day, from 07:00 until 17:30, with three or four timings to Dwejra (which cost 25c each way), depending on the season.

FBY 031 turns in front of the imposing parish church in the San Lawrenz on route 91 on March 26th 2002. The striking application of the vehicle's red bands is clearly in evidence. *Garry Luck*

FBY 051, a Bedford SB with Aquilina body, loads up with tourists who have been visiting Dwejra on 4th August 1998.

ROUTE 14 TO ST LUCIA AND KERCEM

Of all the routes on the island, this route is most difficult for the day-tourist or enthusiast to savour, as it boasts only three morning departures, at 07:00, 09:00 and 10:00, and thereafter only the service at 16:00 which starts from the Industrial Estate. The additional problem is that the three morning departures start at Sabina Square at the far end of Victoria, and not at the Bus Terminus.

Kercem is the village closest to Victoria and Santa Lucija is a suburb. The main road to the villages passes through the upper part of the fertile Lunzjata Valley. However, the route's outward journey uses a rather rough minor road to reach Santa Lucija before returning along the main road to Kercem, where there is the site of 3rd and 4th century Christian catacombs and possibly even earlier Roman baths.

FBY 050 halts in front of the parish church at Kercem on the 10:00 timing on 4th August 2001.

ROUTE 21 TO MARSALFORN

Marsalforn lies on the north coast of Gozo, and is nowadays the busiest of the island's resorts in the summer. Until the development of Mgarr in the 17th century, Marsalforn was the principal harbour for Gozo. The village church is dedicated to St Paul Shipwrecked and dates from 1730. Tradition has it that St Paul set sail from here, after his three-month stay on the Maltese islands.

The direct route to Marsalforn from Victoria descends to a plain overlooked by the strangely shaped conical hill on top of which is the Statue of the Saviour. Islanders once feared that the hill was a dormant volcano (because of its shape) and so built the holy statue on its summit so that it would not dare erupt.

During the summer months (July to September), bus services to Marsalforn are the most intense on the island. Three early timings at 06:00, 06:45 and 07:35 are then followed by departures every three-quarters of an hour from 08:30 until 23:00. Five of the timings, at approximately two-hourly intervals, extend to Qbajjar which is reached along the scenic promenade from Marsalforn village centre. From Qbajjar a short walk to Xwejni reveals a number of saltpans of Roman origin. Winter and spring timetables boast eleven departures during the day roughly every hour, with three extended to Qbajjar.

FBY 035, one of Gozo's two Bristol LHs, has National Bus-style Eastern Coach Works bodywork and is seen taking on passengers at Qjabbar on the 16:45 timing on 31st July, 2001.

ROUTE 25 VICTORIA TO MGARR

This route is operated in accordance with the ferry departures from the harbour at Mgarr. The Gozo Channel Company provides a regular service between Mgarr and Cirkewwa on the northern tip of Malta every day. Buses leave Victoria half an hour before each ferry departure, with the first bus at 05:30. The last bus back from Mgarr varies according to season, but is no later than 20:00, even at the height of the summer tourist season. Two buses are rostered to provide this service each day, with any of the other six buses in service likely to be called upon to provide extra capacity if necessary, especially later on in the afternoons when the day-visitors to Gozo are returning to Malta. During the summer up to 45 departures can take place each day.

The route simply covers the main road between the two termini and takes about a quarter of an hour.

Mgarr is the only gateway to Gozo, apart from the heliport at Ghajnsielem. Overlooking the harbour are Fort Chambray which was built by the Knights of St John in 1749 and the church dedicated to Our Lady of Lourdes. The harbour itself and nearby marina are a haven for small craft and fishing boats. Ashore there are restaurants and bars. On the busy summer days when coach tours for holiday-makers from Malta are arranged, maybe as many as thirty of the island's coach fleet can be seen here awaiting passengers mid-morning.

This view represents a happy coincidence of vehicle number and route, for here is FBY 025, a Bedford SB with Aquilina body, on route 25, having just arrived at Mgarr from Victoria with passengers for the ferry back to Cirkewwa on Easter Monday afternoon 2000.

ROUTE 42/43 TO NADUR, QALA, GHAJNSIELEM, XEWKIJA AND RAMLA

This route runs to the easternmost villages of the island and, in summer, serves another of the popular tourist areas, Ramla Bay, on the north coast. There are fifteen departures a day, at half-hourly intervals from 07:30 until 11:00 (which is the first of the day to serve Ramla), then an 11:45 departure which does not return to Victoria. During the afternoon, two timings serve Ramla, there is then the 15:45 timing serving the Industrial Estate, followed by early evening departures on the hour at 17:00, 18:00 and 19:00 with Ramla Bay served finally by the 18:00 timing.

From Victoria, the route leads out of town serving Nadur directly via the road past the Gozo Racecourse, or else via Xewkija ("the place where thistles grow") which is famous for its Rotunda church. This parish church, dedicated to St John the Baptist, was begun in 1951 and completed thirty years later, and was built by voluntary labour with the construction costs paid for by weekly contributions from the 3,500 villagers. The dome claims to be the third largest unsupported dome in the world, after St Paul's Cathedral in London and St Peter's in Rome. The church was constructed around and over its eighteenth century predecessor which was dismantled only after the new Rotunda was fit to be used towards the end of its construction time.

FBY 053 passes in front of the parish church at Nadur on the 13:15 timing on 4th August 2001.

FBY 026 sets off from Ramla Bay on the 15:00 timing on 30th July 1999.

Gozo heliport is next seen. Close by is an old farmhouse, now renovated as the home of Gozo Heritage, an audio-visual pageant of 7,000 years of the history of the island. The bus turns left off the main road to serve Ghajnsielem with its great neo-Gothic church, begun in 1922 and finished over half a century later, in 1978, when the parish priest won the National Lottery and donated Lm10,000 for its new altar. The church's spire stands out amongst all the other church domes in the village.

A steep climb round hairpin bends brings the bus to Nadur, which overlooks the ferry terminal at Mgarr. Nadur has a very fitting name considering this lofty position, for it means "to keep guard". The Baroque church, dedicated to St Peter and St Paul, was begun in 1760 and was still being added to at the turn of the twentieth century. Also to be seen in Nadur is the Maritime Museum. Here there is a display of model sailing ships, naval emblems and uniforms covering 300 years of history, all of which was amassed by Kelinu Grima. The Kenuna Tower is another landmark, built by the British in 1848, on a spot where warning bonfires were lit during the time when the Knights of St John held sway. Its purpose was originally to serve as a telegraph link between Gozo and Malta.

Qala is the easternmost village on Gozo; its name means "sheltered harbour", and like Xaghra, boasts working windmills and a Baroque church.

From here the descent to Ramla Bay provides wonderful views of the red-gold sands of the bay, fertile meadows, and on the hill opposite, Xaghra. Holidaymakers come to this bay for the day, and as with the route to Dwejra, the journey costs 25c, whereas all other trips on the island cost 15c. From Ramla the bus climbs up the hill to Xaghra and returns to Victoria via route 64.

ROUTE 50/51 TO SANNAT AND MUNXAR

This is another of the shorter routes from Victoria to two villages about two kilometres distant, which are served four times during the morning, and then at 16:00 for the workers' service from the Industrial Estate and then the final departure at 17:15.

The route from Victoria is southwards along the direct main road to Sannat. This village boasts a church begun in 1718 with a fine altarpiece by a local artist, Stefano Errardi. Near the village are more prehistoric remains, the L-Imramma Temple and three dolmens. In Sannat the bus may pass the church and travel up to Ta' Cenc to serve a large hotel complex built around a *palazzo* of the 17th century, which regularly features in lists of the world's top hotels. The precipitous cliffs nearby are over 400 feet high. Returning through Sannat, the bus bears left to travel along a more minor road to Munxar, from where there is again easy access to the cliff-tops. The bus then returns directly to Victoria, with the whole journey taking less than a quarter of hour.

The daily departure times of this route are such that it is interworked with route 87 to Xlendi.

FBY 042 pauses in the village square at Sannat one afternoon in late March 2001. *Garry Luck*

ROUTE 64/65 TO XAGHRA

This route runs directly to Xaghra, a hilltop village whose name refers to the wilderness of the hill before the area was built upon. On leaving the bus terminus at Victoria, the bus travels down the main road, bearing left at the first roundabout along a dual-carriageway lined with oleanders (Gozo's national flower). A steep ascent involving two sharp (almost hairpin) bends brings the bus into Xaghra.

Many of the holiday-makers using this route will have come to Xaghra to visit the Ggantija Temples. These prehistoric temples date from 3600-3000 BC and are recognised as the oldest free-standing structures in the world. There are two temples with a common façade, but each has its own entrance. Local legend tells that the giantess Sansuna carried on her head the huge stones used for building the temples.

Nearby is the Ta' Kola Windmill which the bus will pass by as it makes a short circuit of the roads near the Temples. The windmill was built in 1725 and was named after one of the first millers to work it. Still in working condition, it was used throughout the Second World War to provide wheat for the islanders.

There are thirteen timings of the route each day, at 45-minute intervals throughout the morning with two afternoon departures, the workers' service and then three on the hour - at 17:00, 18:00 and 19:00. The 09:45 timing extends to Tan Nazzarenu on the eastern edge of the village along the road leading to Ramla Bay. The 15:15 includes a service to Marsalforn, and the final departure of the day is one of those designated "not to return to Victoria". No Sunday service is provided.

ROUTE 87 TO XLENDI

Lying on the south-west coast of Gozo, Xlendi is a typical fishing village, and in the summer, a favourite resort for holiday-makers. The route from Victoria passes through Fontana where there is a natural fresh-water spring (hence the name of the village), still in use today by local washerwomen. In the 19th century many of the fishermen at Xlendi lived in Fontana, and income from their catches went towards the building costs of the parish church.

On leaving Fontana the bus begins its descent to Xlendi and the terminus is amongst the palm-trees behind the waterfront. Cliffs border the inlet forming the village harbour, with Xlendi Tower, built in 1650, as a protection against naval attacks and capable of withstanding gunpowder shots, overlooking the harbour. The village, like Marsalforn, is a popular lunchtime destination for some of coach-trips to the island.

There are twelve departures to Xlendi each day, including Sunday, during the summer months, mostly on the hour. The spring timetable boasts only six or seven timings, however.

FBY 032 pauses in front of the Ta' Kola windmill in Xaghra, as local passengers return home on the 13:15 timing from Victoria on 31st July 2001.

FBY 048 is the less common combination of Bristol LH chassis and Plaxton body. It is parked under the trees at Xlendi terminus, waiting for its day-trippers to return from lunch, on 12th April 2001.

SUNDAY BUS SERVICES ON GOZO

The Sunday bus routes, which operate on Public Holidays too, provide a few timings on some of the routes, but only during the morning, catering primarily for church services.

There are nine departures, and in the summer of 2002 this diagram of services was current:

07:00	Route 42/43	Victoria – Nadur – Qala – Ghajnsielem – Xewkija - Victoria
07:30	Route 64/65	Victoria – Xaghra – Xewkija roundabout - Victoria
09:00	Route 42/43	Victoria – Xewkija – Ghajnsielem – Qala – Nadur – Victoria
10:00	Route 64/65	Victoria – Xewkija roundabout – Xaghra – Victoria
11:00	Route 42/43	Victoria – Xewkija – Ghajnsielem – Qala – Nadur
11:30	Route 91	Victoria – Gharb – St Peter – St Lawrence – Victoria
11:30	Route 91	Victoria – Zebbug – Ghasri – Victoria
11:45	Route 50/51	Victoria – Ta' Cawla – Sannat – Munxar

In addition, route 25 Victoria to Mgarr (Gozo Ferries terminal) operates in accordance with the ferry timetable.

FBY 005 proudly proclaims its Castrosua bodywork as it waits for the final few tourists to return after their lunch-stop at Marsalforn on 12th April 2001.

UNSCHEDULED BUSES ON MALTA

The unscheduled buses on Malta are the tour coaches of the island. Indeed, for most tourists arriving by plane at Luqa Airport, a tour coach is the first PSV that they are likely to see and use. Totalling almost 150, these coaches provide the journeys between the holiday resorts and Luqa Airport for holidaymakers, and, of course, the daily tours around the island, and connections from hotels to the Gozo Ferry at Cirkewwa for day-trippers to Malta's smaller neighbour. The age profile of these coaches ranges from some AEC Reliances with Plaxton bodywork imported second-hand from Britain which are nearly 35 years old, to the modern coaches on Volvo and Scania chassis with bodywork built by Ghabbour in Egypt and Irizar in Spain, and the most recent new arrival, the King Long coach. In addition there are individual coaches of especial interest, such as the Leyland Tiger Cub with Maltese-built Brincat body – a 1952 chassis with a 1972 body, or the MAN/Caetano coach with only 35 seats and an ERF Trailblazer with a Camo body.

Until the early 1980s coaches on Malta bore an all-over cream livery. Many, if not all of them, carried locally built bodywork. The livery was then changed to blue and cream. As newer coaches arrived on the island, many of the cream-coloured coaches were cascaded down to operate as route buses on the island. The foregoing route bus fleet-list clearly indicates this change in use vehicle by vehicle.

During 1986 and 1987 the main influx of coaches from the United Kingdom began. They too were painted in the blue and cream livery, and a few of them can still be seen on the island nowadays.

The latest brand-new arrival on Malta amongst the coaches is the King Long vehicle which arrived in July 2001. Originally in service in an all-over white livery, it had received its SMS Tours logo by 21st August that year, when it was seen in Triq il-Kbira in Sliema. *Nick Eyles*

ACY 915 now boasts KopTaCo connections, whilst still retaining its owner's livery and styling. Its Ventura ancestry is indicated on the front, too. It was parked safely amongst road-works at the roundabout at the top of Selmun Hill near Mellieha, at the junction with the Mellieha bypass on the evening of 26th March 2002. *Garry Luck*

Many of these early imports were Plaxton-bodied coaches without opening side windows. They soon became unpopular with passengers, as they offered little or no accessible ventilation, especially to offset the high average summer temperatures on the island. Consequently individual owners installed air-conditioning to alleviate the problems caused by the heat on board these coaches.

Until the early 1990s the vast majority of the coaches had remained "anonymous" – that is, they carried no indication of their owner's name or fleetname.

But a gradual change then took place, as more and more of the coaches — still in the blue and cream livery — appeared with their operator's name proudly displayed. In 1995 a de-restriction in coach liveries was introduced which allowed coach operators to devise their own liveries, as the authorities wished to make the island's coaching scene brighter. Some of the larger coaching firms were very quick to seize the opportunity to individualise their fleet. Garden of Eden was the first company to set the trend.

Tourism on Malta had obviously grown over the years, and the PTA recognised the need for a larger coaching fleet to cope with the ever-increasing demands of the tourist companies. So these changes coincided with the importation of the Plaxton Paramount coaches from Britain.

The PTA regulates the unscheduled buses – at arm's length. The coach firms range in size from the larger fleets of Garden of Eden, Zarb, Cancu and Paramount Garages to the family-owned businesses with only two, three or four coaches, such as Arthur and John's, Bonu Coaches and Oxley Coaches.

LCY 004 awaits passengers at Vittoriosa during September 2002. This Morris Commercial Brincat was rebuilt in 1991, and now, seating seventeen, is confined to sightseeing duties with Nazzareno Abela of Zejtun. *Michael Lee*

In between there is KopTaCo, a co-operative of smaller operators who, so as to benefit from the economies of scale, have joined together to help to pay for new coaches. KopTaCo was formed in 1996, at the time when the most recent large batches of new coaches (those with Ghabbour and Irizar bodywork) were imported. Since then some of the smaller coach firms have opted in and out of the co-operative, the newest recruit being Ventura in 2001. KopTaCo coaches carry a corporate purple and white livery, but there has been a recent trend for the individual firms within KopTaCo to introduce their own colours whilst maintaining the corporate styling. The larger firms, like Garden of Eden and Cancu, are obviously under the control of the PTA, but their sphere of influence enables each of them to pursue its own policies, and to acquire the licences of other operators.

Apart from these 150 or so coaches, there are three idiosyncratic smaller vehicles which are 17-seaters. With registrations LCY 002, 003 and 004, they were built for Captain Morgan Tours (a leading cruise operator on Malta) who used them on a tourist route from close by their moorings at Sliema Ferry to the Three Cities. These three coaches were built in the style of the island's original 1920s coaches; whilst they look old, their bodywork was in fact built by Brincat as recently as 1991 and 1992, but built on old car or lorry chassis. Cancu now owns them and they still operate the same route during the main holiday months, twice daily, at 11:30 and 14:30, from Sliema Ferry.

UNSCHEDULED BUSES (TOUR COACHES)

In this section the second line of data for each coach gives details of the wording to be seen included within the vehicle's livery.

JCY 850	Dennis Javelin 11SDL1905	Plaxton Paramount 3200 III	C53F	1/89	6/93	Leone Grech, Mosta Paramount Coaches
KCY 851	Ford R1114	Caetano Alpha	C53F	11/79	4/86	Victor Muscat, Naxxar KopTaCo Coaches
JCY 852	Dennis Javelin 11SDA1906	Plaxton Paramount 3200 II	C53F	1/90	5/93	Leone Grech, Mosta Paramount Coaches
KCY 853	Bedford YNT	Plaxton Paramount II	C53F	8/85	by 10/91	Dalli Bros., Gzira Welcome Garage
ACY 854	Bedford YMT	Unicar	C53F	7/79	by 8/86	Nazzareno Abela, Zetjun Cancu on KopTaCo colours
KCY 855	Bedford YMT	Duple Dominant II	C53F	1/80	by 8/86	Charles Zammit, Mosta Garden of Eden
LCY 856	Bedford YNT	Plaxton Paramount 3200 II	C53F	5/85	by 12/91	John Galea, Balzan Arthur and John's
LCY 857	Bedford YMT	Van Hool McArdle	C53F	5/78	by 1/87	Carmen Agius, Qormi (No identification on the vehicle)
LCY 858	Bedford YMT	Duple Dominant II	C53F	6/80	by 3/86	John Galea, Balzan Arthur and John's
ACY 859	Bedford YMT	Plaxton Supreme III	C53F	6/77	by 10/86	Joseph Mary Farrugia, Mosta KopTaCo Coaches
LCY 860	Dennis Javelin GX	Plaxton Excalibur	C53F	1997	c6/00	Leone Grech, Mosta Paramount Coaches *carried within Plaxton demonstration livery used prior to its importation to Malta.*
BCY 861	Optimal	Scarnif	C53F	by 10/01	by 11/01	Nazzareno Abela, Zejtun Cancu
BCY 862	Volvo B10M-62	Plaxton Première 350	C50F	6/96	2002	Nazzareno Abela, Zejtun Cancu Supreme
ACY 863	Leyland Tiger TRCL10/3ARZM	Plaxton Paramount 3500 III	C53F	1/91	by 4/98	Angelo Spiteri, Ghaxaq Garden of Eden
KCY 864	Bedford YMT	Plaxton Supreme IV Express	C53F	1/80	by 8/66	Carmel k/a Charles Dalli Gzira "Supreme Express" (on front)
JCY 865	Volvo B10M-62	Plaxton Première 350	C48FT	5/96	2002	Dalli Bros. Welcome Garage
ACY 866	Volvo B10M-62	Plaxton Première 350	C53F	5/96	3/01	Anthony Grima, Mellieha KopTaCo
LCY 867	Bedford YMT	Plaxton Supreme III Express	C53F	3/77	by 10/86	Charles Gauchi, Mosta KopTaCo

JCY 850, Y-0850, F666 PAY	Snowdon, Easington Colliery
KCY 851, Y-0851, CNY 333V	Eynon, Trimsaran
JCY 852, Y-0852, G966 WNR	Dunnet, Keiss
KCY 853, Y-0853, C350 FBO	Avondale, Rothwell
ACY 854, Y-0854, EBC 567T	Winson, Loughborough, 1
KCY 855, Y-0855, EHE 225V	Anderson, Westerhope
LCY 856, Y-0856, B624 DDW	GP Travel, London
LCY 857, Y-0857, TOH 746S	Arnold, Tamworth
LCY 858, Y-0858, HVO 20V	Clarke, Burbage
ACY 859, Y-0859, SBH 107R	K Line, Huddersfield
LCY 860	Demonstrator in Hong Kong (Stored from 4/99 to c6/00)
BCY 861	New
BCY 862, N242 HWX	Wallace Arnold, Leeds
ACY 863, H381 TNG	Elsey, Gosberton
KCY 864, Y-0864, KBH 856V	Clarkes of London
JCY 865, N212 HWX, 96-D-25736	Cityliner, Port Glasgow (originally Bus Eireann, VP13)
ACY 866, N758 BNU	Dunn–Line, Nottingham
LCY 867, Y-0867, PNK 150R	Scotland & Bates, Appledore

ACY 866 is one of the latest coaches to arrive on the island and still carried an all-over white livery during the summer 2001 season, although it is confidently believed that it will eventually receive the KopTaCo livery. It is seen parked at Valletta Bus Terminus, with BCY 913, Cancu's Bedford YNT behind, on 7th August 2001.

LCY 857 is the only Van Hool-bodied coach on Malta and is seen here at Marsaxlokk harbour waiting for its passengers to return from visiting the village, on 29th July 2001.

BCY 876 is the most recently rebuilt coach by Scarnif. It is seen at Cirkewwa Ferry, still without the application of fleet name and livery, as its passengers alight to cross over to Gozo for the day on 4th August 2001.

JCY 868	Bedford YNT	Plaxton Paramount 3200 III	C53F	3/87	c4/90	Leone Grech, Mosta
						Paramount Garages
JCY 869	Bedford YNT	Plaxton Paramount 3200	C54F	6/84	by 7/87	Leone Grech, Mosta
		Paramount Garages or Thompson (*This vehicle carries transferable boards on its sides*)				
KCY 870	Bedford YMT	Duple Dominant II	C53F	4/79	4/88	Carmel Zammit, Mosta
						KopTaCo
CCY 871	Bedford YMT	Duple Dominant II	C53F	5/80	by 3/87	Saviour Borg, Msida
						Oxley Coaches; Dansk FolkeFerie
KCY 872	Bedford YMT	Duple Dominant II	C53F	8/77	by 3/86	Paul Muscat, Naxxar
						KopTaCo
KCY 873	Bedford YMT	Duple Dominant II	C53F	3/79	by 10/87	Emanuel Vella, Qormi
						KopTaCo
LCY 874	Ford R1114	Duple Dominant II	C53F	5/78	by 8/86	Joseph Bonnici, Naxxar
						(*No identification on the vehicle*)
KCY 875	Bedford YMT	Duple Dominant II	C53F	4/78	by 3/86	Joseph Saliba, Zurrieq
						Nimrod Coaches
BCY 876	Bedford YMT	Scarnif	C53F	8/78	by 5/87	Mario Sultana, Gzira
						(*No identification on the vehicle*)
KCY 877	Bedford YMT	Plaxton Supreme IV	C53F	12/79	4/87	Mario Sultana, Gzira
						Sultana
ACY 878	Bedford YMT	Caetano Alpha	C53F	10/79	by 8/86	Kevin Muscat, Gharghur
						KopTaCo

JCY 868, Y-0868, D371 KDB   Bullock, Cheadle
JCY 869, Y-0869, A111 MAC   Harry Shaw, Coventry
KCY 870, Y-0870, BRY 63T   Mundy, Orpington
CCY 871, Y-0871, GPA 631V   Arrowline, Hayes
KCY 872, Y-0872, UTV 813S   Rodgers, Langwith
KCY 873, Y-0873, UWH 694T   Bailey, Kirkby
LCY 874, Y-0874, TPC 251S   Brindley and Smith, West Bromwich
KCY 875, Y-0875, YHJ 169S   Poulson, Copford
BCY 876, Y-0876, YPB 822T   Grimshaw, Burnley
KCY 877, Y-0877, KDH 831V   Bridges, Saham Toney
ACY 878, Y-0878, KUB 962V   Aris, Long Hanborough

LCY 895, a Bedford YMT with Duple Dominant II bodywork, is one of Schembri's coaches. It is seen at Cirkewwa on 16th April, Easter Monday, 2001.

KCY 879	AEC Reliance 6U3ZR	Plaxton Supreme IV	C53F	1/79	by 7/87	Rennie Zammit, Mosta Silver Star
CCY 880	Bedford YMT	Plaxton Supreme IV	C53F	4/80	3/86	*Owner unknown*, Naxxar Hello Tourist
BCY 881	Leyland Royal Tiger PSU1/15	Brincat (1972)	C40F	1952	7/72	Charles Pace, Gzira (*No identification on the vehicle*)
JCY 882	Volvo B10M-60	Plaxton Première 350	C48FT	5/92	7/01	Emmanuel Zarb, San Gwann Zarb Coaches
JCY 883	AEC Reliance ETS	Plaxton Supreme IV (1979)	C53F	5.67	4/87	Emmanuel Zarb, San Gwann Zarb Coaches
KCY 884	Optimal Leyland	Scarnif	C53F	2001	2001	Emmanuel Zarb, San Gwann Zarb Coaches
LCY 885	Leyland Tiger TRCTL11/2R	Plaxton Paramount 3200	C53F	1/84	by 10/91	Joseph Zarb, Naxxar Zarb Coaches, Express
ACY 886	Bedford YMT	Duple Dominant II	C53F	1/80	3/87	Jane Sammut, Luqa Morin Coaches
ACY 887	Bedford YMT	Scarnif (1996)	C53F	1980	by 8/86	Anthony Zahra, San Gwann First Coaches
KCY 888	Ford R1114	Caetano Alpha	C53F	11/80	4/88	Paul Muscat, Naxxar KopTaCo
KCY 889	Dennis Javelin 11SDA1906	Plaxton Paramount 3200 III	C53F	3/88	by 4/94	Carmelo Aquilina, Msida Cancu (*but in former owner's livery*)
KCY 890	Bedford YNT	Plaxton Paramount 3200 II	C53F	2/87	6/91	Leone Grech, Mosta Paramount Garages

KCY 879, Y-0879, BGY 583T — New Enterprise, Tonbridge
CCY 880, Y-0880, LVS 435V — Reliance, Newbury, 170 (*This vehicle still carries the former standard blue and cream coach livery*)

BCY 881, Y-0881, Y-1581, A-0215, 215, LUF 826 — Wimpey, London W6
JCY 882, OIL 5640, J716 CWT — Associated Motorways, Harlow
JCY 883, Y-0883, CPM 520T, HOD 39E — Thomas, West Ewell, (*This vehicle was rebuilt from AEC Reliance 2U3RA Duple Northern in 1978 and rebodied in 1979*)

KCY 884 — New
LCY 885, Y-0885, A633 XFM, 614 BWU, A423 LRJ — Barry Cooper, Stockton Heath
ACY 886, Y-0886, FUJ 920V — Whittle, Kidderminster
ACY 887, Y-0887, EHL 922V — Excelsior, Dinnington, (*This vehicle was rebodied in 1996*)
KCY 888, Y-0888, NAY 428W — Cedric, Wivenhoe
KCY 889, Y-0889, E270 AJL — Hornsby, Ashby
KCY 890, Y-0890, 9424 RU, D370 KDB — County, Brentwood

BCY 881 is one of island's coaches not often seen in service. It is seen awaiting passengers in Triq il-Torri in Sliema during the Easter weekend, 2001. *Nick Eyles*

KCY 891	Ford R1114	Plaxton Supreme IV	C53F	2/79	5/87	Anthony Grima, Mellieha
						KopTaCo (but with Ventura livery)
LCY 892	Bedford YMT	Plaxton Supreme IV	C53F	3/79	by 10/87	Salvino Farrugia, Paola
						KopTaCo
LCY 893	Bedford YMT	Plaxton Supreme IV	C53F	10/80	11/88	Godwin Farrugia, Mosta
						KopTaCo
ACY 894	Bedford YMT	Duple Dominant II	C53F	9/77	by 4/88	Unknown
						(*KopTaCo colours, but no identification on the vehicle*)
LCY 895	Bedford YMT	Duple Dominant II	C53F	5/78	by 3/86	Joseph Schembri, Siggiewi
						Schembri Coaches
LCY 896	AEC Reliance 6U3ZR	Plaxton Supreme III	C53F	3/77	by 4/89	Mario Sultana, Gzira
						KopTaCo
LCY 897	Bedford YNT	Plaxton Paramount 3200 II	C53F	11/85	by 10/91	Mario Sultana, Gzira
						Sultana
KCY 898	Bedford YMT	Plaxton Supreme IV	C53F	11/78	2/87	Joseph Zarb, San Pawl il-Bihar
						(*No identification on the vehicle*)
JCY 899	Bedford YMT	Duple Dominant II	C53F	4/78	by 8/86	Jason Spiteri, Gzira
						Garden of Eden
LCY 900	Ford R1114	Caetano Alpha	C53F	1/80	by 8/86	Andrew Spiteri, Luqa
						V. S. and Sons Coaches
BCY 901	Ford R1114	Scarnif (1998)	C53F	4/79	by 10/86	Salvu Abela, Zejtun
						Robert Arrigo and Sons Ltd

KCY 891, Y-0891, WHC 538T
LCY 892, Y-0892, CEL 104T
LCY 893, Y-0893, NJU 3W
ACY 894, Y-0894, UAY 214S
LCY 895, Y-0895, UUT 786S
LCY 896, Y-0896, BCX 679R, VBR 334, TWY 962R
LCY 897, Y-0897, C432 HHL
KCY 898, Y-0898, CRW 517T
JCY 899, Y-0899, VNT 1S
LCY 900, Y-0900, HAY 800V
BCY 901, Y-0901, YCF 966T

WHM, Little Walthorn
Winson, Loughborough
Beckett, Horwood
New Enterprise, Tonbridge
Arrowline, Hayes
Smith, Thirsk
Wainfleet, Nuneaton
Bailey, Kirkby
Arleen, Peasedown
Globe, Barnsley
Reliance, Newbury, 160 (*This vehicle was rebodied in1998*)

CCY 904 was parked at Qawra bus terminus at about noon on 29th March 2002.

BCY 902	Leyland Leopard PSU3C/4R	Plaxton Paramount 3200 II	C53F	12/76	4/91	Catherine Abela, Zejtun Cancu Supreme
ACY 903	AEC Reliance 6U3ZR	Duple Dominant II	C53F	8/79	by 1/87	Andrew Spiteri, Luqa Cancu Supreme
CCY 904	Bedford YMT	Plaxton Supreme Express	C53F	4/78	by 10/87	Saviour Abela, Birzebbugia Swallow Garage
JCY 905	Leyland Royal Tiger PSU1/13	Paramount Garage	C41F	5/53	5/75	Leone Grech, Mosta Paramount Garages
ACY 906	Bedford YMT	Duple Dominant II	C53F	1/79	by 10/87	Joseph Pace, Qormi Cancu Supreme
LCY 907	King Long	King Long	C49F	7/01	7/01	Nazzareno Abela, Zejtun SMS Tours (Mifsud and Sons)
ACY 908	Volvo B10M-60	Plaxton Excalibur	C50F	4/94	10/2	Andrew Abela, Zejtun Cancu Supreme
ACY 909	Scania K93CRB	Plaxton Paramount 3200 III	C53F	4/91	by 4/95	Jane Sammut, Luqa Morin Coaches
LCY 910	Volvo B10M-56	Plaxton Paramount 3500 II	C53F	3/85	by 10/91	John Galea, Balzan Arthur and John's
ACY 911	Volvo B10M-60	Plaxton Première 350	C53F	3/93	1/02	Mario Abela, Zejtun Cancu Supreme
ACY 912	Volvo B10M-62	Plaxton Première 350	C50FT	3/95	c4/00	Nazzareno Abela, Zejtun Cancu Supreme

BCY 902, Y-0902, 961 PEH, TGD 218R	Stevenson, Uttoxeter, 9
ACY 903, Y-0903, LBD 929V	Vaughan, Salford
CCY 904, Y-0904, WRY 90S	Don, Dunmow
JCY 905, Y-0905, Y-1605, A-1982, 1982, GUH 462	Skey, Sywell
(*This vehicle was rebodied in-house by Paramount Garages during 1996*)	
ACY 906, Y-0906, AUJ 734T	New Enterprise, Tonbridge
(*This vehicle still carries the former blue and cream coach livery*)	
LCY 907	New
ACY 908, L930 NWW	Smith, Market Harborough
ACY 909, Y-2501, H926 DRJ	Shearings, 926
LCY 910, Y-0910, B367 RHC, NDY 820, B191 XJD	Rambler, Hastings
ACY 911, K624FEC	Fishwick, Leyland
ACY 912, M39 KAX	Bluebird Buses

CCY 920 is owned by one of the smaller coach companies on Malta, Bonu Coaches, this name being a corruption of the owner's surname. In immaculate condition, it awaits passengers outside the Bugibba Holiday Complex early in the morning of 27th July 2001.

BCY 913	Bedford YNT	Plaxton Paramount 3200 II	C53F	6/87	by 4/93	Nazzareno Abela, Zejtun
						Cancu Supreme
ACY 914	Ford R1114	Duple Dominant II	C53F	1/77	by 3/87	Anthony Grima, Mellieha
						(No identification on the vehicle)
ACY 915	AEC Reliance ETS	Plaxton Supreme IV (1981)	C53F	7/66	by 3/90	Anthony Grima, Mellieha
						KopTaCo Coaches, Ventura Coaches
BCY 916	Bedford YMT	Duple Dominant II	C53F	4/79	by 8/86	Carmel Abela, Zejtun
						(No identification on the vehicle)
ACY 917	Volvo B10M-62	Plaxton Première 350	C53F	3/95	2001	Nazzareno Abela, Zejtun
						Cancu (In all-over cream livery)
ACY 918	Bedford YMT	Duple Dominant II	C53F	4/77	by 3/86	Mario Abela, Zejtun
						Cancu Supreme - (In all-over white livery without identification)
KCY 919	Ford R1114	Duple Dominant II	C53F	9/79	2/86	Anthony Grima, Mellieha
						KopTaCo
CCY 920	Ford R1114	Plaxton Supreme IV	C53F	4/79	2/86	Paul Debono, San Gwann
						Bonu Coaches
LCY 921	Bedford YMT	Plaxton Supreme IV	C53F	5/80	4/87	Angelo Spiteri, Ghaxaq
						Garden of Eden
LCY 922	Bedford YMT	Duple Dominant II	C53F	4/80	by 3/86	Joseph Mifsud, Gzira
						KopTaCo Coaches

BCY 913, Y-0913, D 384 CFR, BIB 5428, D439 GAD — Bibby, Ingleton

ACY 914, Y-0914, NDK 297R — Kenyon, Bolton (This vehicle still carries the former blue and cream coach livery)

ACY 915, Y-0915, OPD 789W, KHM 5D — Thomas, West Ewell (This vehicle was rebuilt from AEC Reliance 3U2RA Willowbrook and rebodied in 1981)

BCY 916, Y-0916, FKX 275T — Reliance, Newbury
ACY 917, M171EYG, 8980 WA, M103 UWY — Wallace Arnold, Leeds
ACY 918, Y-0918, SNR 632R — Brockbank, Staveley
KCY 919, Y-0919, CYH 801V — Cowie, London N16
CCY 920, Y-0920, AUJ 523T — Wilkinson, Hebburn
LCY 921, Y-0921, UHJ 351V, 5919 RU, MMJ 473V — County, Brentwood
LCY 922, Y-0922, GPA 630V — Arrowline, Hayes

BCY 934 is parked below the walls of St James' Bastion at Porta Reale bus terminus in Valletta on 30th July 2001.

Reg	Chassis	Body				Owner
LCY 923	Optimal	Scarnif	C53F	4/98	4/98	Anthony Zahra, San Gwann
						First Coaches
BCY 924	Bedford YMT	Duple Dominant II Express	C53F	4/79	by 3/86	Emmanuel Cassar, Birzebbugia
						Cancu Supreme
JCY 925	Dennis Javelin 11SDL1905	Plaxton Paramount 3200 III	C53F	1/88	5/93	Leone Grech, Mosta
						Paramount Garages
xCY 926	(This registration has never been issued)					
xCY 927	(This registration has never been issued)					
xCY 928	(This registration has never been issued)					
CCY 929	Dennis Javelin 12SDA1929	Berkhof Excellence 1000	C53F	8/91	1/95	Angelo Spiteri, Ghaxaq
						Garden of Eden
BCY 930	Dennis Javelin 12SDA1929	Berkhof Excellence 1000	C53F	1/92	1/95	Angelo Spiteri, Ghaxaq
						Garden of Eden
BCY 931	Leyland Tiger TRCL10/3RZM	Plaxton 321	C53F	5/91	1/95	Carmelo Abela, Zejtun
						Zarb Coaches
ACY 932	Leyland Tiger TRCL10/3RZM	Plaxton Paramount 3200 III	C53F	1/92	1/95	Emanuel Zarb, Gzira
						Zarb Coaches
BCY 932	Scania K93 CRB	Ghabbour	C55F	11/95	11/95	Charles Borg, Qormi
						Zarb Coaches
BCY 933	Leyland Tiger TRCL10/3ARZM	Plaxton Paramount 3200 III	C53F	10/91	1/95	Carmel Zarb, Gzira
						Zarb Coaches
BCY 934	Leyland Tiger TRCL10/3ARZM	Plaxton 321	C53F	8/91	1/95	Nazzareno Abela, Zejtun
						SMS Holidays; S. Mifsud and Sons Ltd

LCY 923 — New
BCY 924, Y-0924, FKX 272T — C& M, Aintree
JCY 925, Y-0925, E842 EUT — Snowdon, Easington Colliery
xCY 926
xCY 927 — *(Fleet numbers 926, 927 and 928 were originally carried by LCY 002,003, 004 (q.v.). The xCY versions have never been issued)*
xCY 928
CCY 929 Y-0929, J10 BCK — Sanders, Holt
BCY 930, Y-0930, H10 GSM — Sanders, Holt
BCY 931, Y-0931, H2 RAD — Dunn-Line, Nottingham
ACY 932, Y-0932, J385 ARR, J8 DLT — Dunn-Line, Nottingham
BCY 932, Y-2521 — New
BCY 933, Y-0933, J7 DLT — Dunn-Line, Nottingham
BCY 934, Y-0934, J328 PDE, A11 WLS, J47 SNY — Silcox, Pembroke Dock

LCY 948, owned by Garden of Eden, is one of four ERF Trailblazers with Unicar bodywork on Malta. It is seen parked near Paola, outside the walls of the island's prison, on the evening of Good Friday, 2001.

LCY 935	Leyland Tiger TRCL10/3ARZM	Plaxton Paramount 3200 III	C53F	4/92	3/95	Esther Grima, Mellieha KopTaCo
JCY 936	Leyland Tiger TRCL10/3ARZM	Plaxton 321	C53F	8/91	1/95	Victor Muscat, Naxxar KopTaCo Ltd
JCY 937	Leyland Tiger TRCL10/3ARZM	Plaxton 321	C53F	8/91	1/95	Paul Muscat, Naxxar KopTaCo
BCY 938	Leyland Tiger TRCL10/3ARZM	Plaxton Paramount 3500 III	C53F	2/91	1/95	Salvu Abela, Zejtun Cancu Supreme
KCY 939	Volvo B10M-60	Plaxton Paramount 3200 III	C53F	8/92	1/95	Anthony Grima, Mellieha KopTaCo
LCY 940	Leyland Tiger TRCL10/3ARZM	Plaxton Paramount 3500 III	C53F	2/92	1/95	Joseph Abela, Ghaxaq Cancu Supreme
KCY 941	Dennis Javelin 12SDA2117	Plaxton Première 320	C53F	4/93	1/95	Carmelo Aquilina, Msida ATV Tours, with Arriaga Group on rear
ACY 942	Leyland Tiger TRCL10/3ARZM	Plaxton 321	C53F	2/91	1/95	Joseph Farrugia, Mosta KopTaCo
KCY 943	Leyland Tiger TRCL10/3ARZM	Plaxton 321	C53F	2/91	1/95	Salvinu Farrugia, Paola KopTaCo
CCY 944	Leyland Tiger TRBL10/3ARZA	Plaxton Paramount 3200 III	C53F	5/91	4/95	Emanuel Zarb, Gzira Zarb Coaches
BCY 945	Leyland Tiger TR2R62C21Z6/8	Plaxton Paramount 3200 III	C53F	6/91	1/95	Leone Grech, Mosta Paramount Garages

LCY 935, Y-0935, J64 KMR   Ellison, Ashton Keynes
JCY 936, Y-0936, J53 SNY   Evans, Tregaron
JCY 937, Y-0937, J56 SNY   Evans, Tregaron
BCY 938, Y-0938, H210 AKH   Porteous, Anlaby
KCY 939, Y-0939, K6 RAD   Dunn-Line, Nottingham
LCY 940, Y-0940, J780 HAT   Alpha, Hull
KCY 941, Y-0941, K365 HBE, 8227 RH, K119 GFU   Hornsby, Ashby
ACY 942, Y-0942, H331 NNY   Thomas Rhondda
KCY 943, Y-0943. H332 NNY   Thomas Rhondda
CCY 944, Y-0944, H263 GRY   Reliance, Gravesend
BCY 945, Y-0945, H266 GRY   Reliance, Gravesend

KCY 953 is a Scania with Plaxton Paramount 3200 III body owned by Nimrod Coaches. It is seen by the gardens adjoining the entrance to the "Silent City" of Mdina on 7th August 2001.

LCY 946	Leyland Tiger TRCL10/3ARZM	Plaxton Paramount 3200 III	C53F	12/91	1/95	Gabriel Vassallo, Rabat KopTaCo
CCY 947	Leyland Tiger TR2R62C21Z6	Plaxton Paramount 3200 III	C53F	5/91	3/95	William Grech, San Giljan Cancu Supreme
LCY 948	ERF E10 Trailblazer	Unicar	C53F	11/95	11/95	Angelo Spiteri, Ghaxaq Garden of Eden
LCY 949	ERF E10 Trailblazer	Unicar	C53F	11/95	11/95	Emanuel Zarb, Gzira Zarb Coaches, Sharing
ACY 950	Volvo B10M-60	Plaxton Première 350	C53F	4/94	2/95	Catherine Abela, Zejtun Cancu (*In an all-over white livery*)
LCY 951	Scania K93CRB	Plaxton Paramount 3200 III	C53F	2/91	2/95	Josephine Cassar, Qormi Morin Coaches Tourmaster
LCY 952	Scania K93CRB	Plaxton Paramount 3200 III	C53F	4/91	2/95	Joseph Borg, Qormi Morin Coaches
KCY 953	Scania K93CRB	Plaxton Paramount 3200 III	C53F	4/91	2/95	Joseph Saliba, Zurrieq Nimrod Coaches
JCY 954	Volvo B10M-60	Plaxton Paramount 3500 III	C53F	6/90	by 3/95	Mario Sultana, Gzira Sultana
JCY 955	Volvo B10M-60	Plaxton Première 350	C53F	5/92	by 5/95	Maria Sultana, Gzira Sultana
CCY 956	Volvo B10M-60	Plaxton Paramount 3500 III	C54F	3/91	by 4/95	Emanuel Zarb, Gzira Zarb Coaches

LCY 946, Y-0946, J260 MFP	Pullman, Crofty
CCY 947, Y-0947, H265 GRY	Reliance, Gravesend
LCY 948, Y-0948	New
LCY 949, Y-0949	New
ACY 950, Y-0950, L981 ORB	Dunn-Line, Nottingham
LCY 951, Y-2502, H930 DRJ	Shearings, 930
LCY 952, Y-2503, H921 DRJ	Shearings, 921
KCY 953, Y-2504, H923 DRJ	Shearings, 923
JCY 954, Y-2505, H115 NFX, XEL 941, H650 KLJ, G990 FFX	Excelsior, Bournemouth
JCY 955, Y-2506, J433 HDS	Redwing, Camberwell
CCY 956, Y-2507, H617 UWR	Berkeley, Paulton

Malta and Gozo Buses

ACY 964 is one of the minority of smaller coaches on the island. It was parked outside Cancu's premises in Zejtun on 25th March 2002.

JCY 957	Volvo B10M-60	Plaxton Paramount 3500 III	C53F	3/91	by 4/95	Paul Debono, San Gwann Bonu Coaches
ACY 958	Dennis Javelin 12SDA2117	Plaxton Première 320	C53F	4/93	2/95	Leone Grech, Mosta Paramount Garages
BCY 959	Scania K93CRB	Ghabbour	C55F	11/95	11/95	Emanuel Vella, Mgarr KopTaCo Coaches
ACY 960	Scania K93CRB	Ghabbour	C55F	11/95	11/95	Andrew Spiteri, Luqa Magna Mater Holidays
LCY 961	Scania K93CRB	Ghabbour	C55F	11/95	11/95	Joseph Schembri, Siggiewi Schembri
KCY 962	Scania K93CRB	Ghabbour	C55F	11/95	11/95	Andrew Pace, Gzira KopTaCo
BCY 963	Scania K93CRB	Ghabbour	C55F	11/95	11/95	Joseph Zarb, San Pawl Il-Bahar Mysterious Fantasy
ACY 964	MAN 11.190 HOCL-R	Caetano Algarve 2	C35F	c11/95	c11/95	Nazzareno Abela, Zejtun Cancu Supreme Midi
LCY 965	Volvo B10M-62	Plaxton Première 350	C53F	11/93	by 11/99	Angelo Spiteri, Ghaxaq Garden of Eden
ACY 966	Scania K93CRB	Ghabbour	C55F	11/95	11/95	Anthony Zahra, San Gwann First Coaches and Chauffeur Drive
LCY 967	Scania K93CRB	Ghabbour	C55F	11/95	11/95	Angelo Zammit, Mellieha Paramount Garages

JCY 957, Y-2508, H624 UWR	Wallace Arnold, Leeds
ACY 958, Y-2509, K264 FUV	Redwing, Camberwell
BCY 959, Y-2510	New
ACY 960, Y-2511	New
LCY 961, Y-2512	New
KCY 962, Y-2513	New
BCY 963, Y-2514	New
ACY 964, Y-2515	New
LCY 965, L254 UCV	Western National, 2254
ACY 966, Y-2517	New
LCY 967, Y-2518	New

LCY 967 carries Egyptian-built Ghabbour bodywork with striking blue and pink livery of Paramount Coaches. It is parked In Triq Valletta in Paola on Good Friday afternoon 2001, having brought a party of tourists to the town for the Easter festivities taking place there.

LCY 968	Scania K93CRB	Ghabbour	C55F	11/95	11/95	Saviour Borg, Msida
						Dansk FolkeFerie: Oxley Ltd (*at rear*)
KCY 969	Scania K93CRB	Ghabbour	C55F	11/95	11/95	Paul Muscat, Paola
						KopTaCo
ACY 970	Volvo B10M-62	Irizar Century 12.35	C53F	c11/95	c11/95	Raymond Gialanze, Zabbar
						KopTaCo Coaches
ACY 971	Volvo B10M-62	Irizar Century 12.35	C53F	c11/95	c11/95	George Caruana, Tarxien
						Cancu (*at front*); George's (*at rear*)
JCY 972	Volvo B10M-62	Irizar Century 12.35	C53F	1/96	1/96	Joseph Calleja, St Julians
						(*No identification on the vehicle*)
KCY 973	Bedford YMT	Duple Dominant II	C53F	7/80	10/86	Angelo Spiteri, Ghaxaq
						Garden of Eden
ACY 974	Volvo B10M-62	Irizar Century 12.35	C53F	c11/95	c11/95	Leone Grech, Mosta
						Paramount Garages
LCY 975	Volvo B10M-62	Irizar Century 12.35	C53F	c11/95	c11/95	Victor Spiteri, Luqa
						Century Coaches
JCY 976	Volvo B10M-62	Irizar Century 12.35	C53F	c11/95	c11/95	Dalli Bros. Ltd, Gzira
						Welcome Garage Cityliner
LCY 977	Volvo B10M-62	Irizar Century 12.35	C53F	c11/95	c11/95	Joseph Zammit, Mosta
						Zarb
LCY 978	Volvo B10M-62	Irizar Century 12.35	C53F	c11/95	c11/95	Charles Zammit, Mosta
						CRJ Coaches

LCY 968, Y-2519	New
KCY 969, Y-2520	New
ACY 970, Y-2522	New
ACY 971, Y-2523	New
JCY 972, Y- 2524	New
KCY 973, Y-0909, MMJ 541V	Tourmaster, Dunstable
ACY 974, Y-2526	New
LCY 975, Y-2527	New
JCY 976, Y-2528	New
LCY 977, Y-2529	New
LCY 978, Y-2530	New

KCY 979	Volvo B10M-62	Irizar Century 12.35	C53F	c11/95	c11/95	Paul Vella, Mosta
						Silver Star
ACY 980	Volvo B10M-62	Irizar Century 12.35	C53F	c11/95	c11/95	Edward Pace, Gzira
						Cancu (but in former owner's colours)
ACY 981	ERF E10 Trailblazer	Unicar	C53F	c11/95	c11/95	Emanuel Zarb, Sliema
						Zarb Coaches
LCY 982	MAN 11.190 HOCL-R	Caetano Algarve 2	C53F	c11/95	c11/95	Josephine Abela, Ghaxaq
						Cancu Supreme
LCY 983	ERF E10 Trailblazer	Unicar	C53F	c11/95	c11/95	John Galea, Balzan
						Arthur and John's Coaches
CCY 984	MAN 11.190 HOCL-R	Berkhof Excellence 1000 Mid	C35F	12/95	12/95	Emanuel Zarb, Gzira
						Zarb Coaches
ACY 985	ERF E10 Trailblazer	Camo	C53F	1/96	1/96	Kevin Muscat, Gharghur
						KopTaCo Coaches
ACY 986	Volvo B10M-62	Plaxton Première 350	C55F	1/96	1/96	Esther Grima, Mellieha
						KopTaCo Coaches
xCY 987	This registration is currently not in use					
JCY 988	Dennis Javelin 12SDA2161	Plaxton Excalibur	C53F	1/96	1/96	Leone Grech, Mosta
						Paramount Garages
JCY 989	Dennis Javelin 12SDA2161	Plaxton Excalibur	C53F	1/96	1/96	Leone Grech, Mosta
						Paramount Garages
JCY 990	Dennis Javelin 12SDA2159	Plaxton Excalibur	C53F	12/95	12/95	Leone Grech, Mosta
						Paramount Garages
CCY 991	Scania K93CRB	Ghabbour	C55F	11/95	11/95	C. Bezzini, Maghtab
						KopTaCo Coaches
CCY 992	MAN 11.190 HOCL-R	Berkhof Excellence 1000 Midi	C35F	by 5/96	by 5/96	Godwin Farrugia, Mosta
						KopTaCo
LCY 001	Mercedes Benz OHL 1684	Irizar Century 12.35	C53FT	10/96	10/96	Leone Grech, Mosta
						Mercedes Benz
CCY 002	MAN 11.190 HOCL-R	Berkhof Excellence 1000 Midi	C35F	by 10/96	by 10/96	Nazarene Abela, Zejtun
						Silver Star

The following three vehicles have rebuilt bodies in the style of the original coaches on the island during the 1920s. They provide a twice-daily tourist service from Sliema Ferry to the Three Cities.

LCY 002	Bedford WLB	Brincat (1991)	B17R	1932	1/91	Nazzareno Abela, Zejtun
						Fom ir Rih
LCY 003	Chevrolet n/c	Brincat (1991)	B17R	by 12/39	by 5/92	Nazzareno Abela, Zejtun
						Mensija
LCY 004	Mercedes n/c	Brincat (1991)	B17R	by 12/39	1/91	Nazzareno Abela, Zejtun
						Melita

KCY 979, Y-2531	New
ACY 980, Y-2532	New
ACY 981, Y-2533	New
LCY 982, Y-2535	New
LCY 983, Y-2536	New
CCY 984, Y-2538	New
ACY 985	New
ACY 986	New
xCY 987	
JCY 988	New
JCY 989	New
JCY 990	New
CCY 991, Y-2525	New
CCY 992	New
LCY 001	New
CCY 002	New
LCY 002, Y-0926	Of unknown origin
LCY 003, Y-0928, 2655	Ex-lorry chassis
LCY 004, Y-0927, 3295	Ex-lorry chassis

ACY 917, one of Cancu's latest additions to the fleet, is parked at Rabat, near to one of the entrances to the "Quiet City" of Mdina, on 8th August 2001.

ACY 985 is a unique coach on Malta, as it alone carries a Camo body. Its fleet colours show one of the several colour variations of the KopTaCo livery to be seen. The coach is on lay-over in Valletta Bus Terminus, on 2nd August 2001.

A BRIEF HISTORY OF SOME OF THE COACH FIRMS.

Guiseppi (or Joseph) Spiteri, the father of the firm's present Chairman, Angelo, founded **Garden of Eden Coach Company** on leap-year day, 29th February 1932. The first vehicle operated was a Chevrolet coach with fourteen seats, numbered 2315, which was used on the route to Cospicua. This vehicle is fondly remembered by the firm and features in much of their publicity. A Diamond 'T' route-bus with 29 seats was purchased next; number 2315 was transferred to it, as is the practice. Some time later a Reo with a Schembri body joined the fleet. It was numbered 973 and was used as a private bus for hire. A Bedford OB, the origins and early history of which are unknown to the family, was the next bus purchased, with the registration J-4792. It is still stored on the company's premises.

Angelo succeeded his father as director of the firm on 7th July 1968. In his free time he set about building a bus for the fleet by himself. Angelo then converted, in-house, their Dodge route bus with Casha and then Tonna bodywork, number 2575, to a private coach. A Plaxton Supreme IV was imported as 1917 and later received number 863.

The company introduced the first minibus to Malta, which was a Commer 22-seater with a body built in-house again, and which was numbered 47185. When in service it carried passengers free of charge as its dimensions contravened the law governing such vehicles.

Garden of Eden continued to update their coach fleet, purchasing a number of coaches from Reliance of Newbury. Jason Camilleri, Angelo's son-in-law, recalls how he drove what became coach 863 all the way from Newbury to Reggio in southern Italy.

J-4792 is parked in Garden of Eden's underground garage with Angelo Spiteri standing alongside. *TWJ collection, courtesy of Angelo Spiteri.*

Yet another coach at Paola on Good Friday 2001 was JCY 955, one of Sultana's Volvo vehicles with Plaxton Première bodywork, in Sultana's own livery.

In 1995 the company took advantage of the government's "offer" which enabled coach owners to purchase one new bus for each bus permit owned. Consequently Dennis Javelins CCY 929 and BCY 930 were bought from England. Twelve months later two brand-new additions to the fleet arrived in the form of an ERF Trailblazer with Unicar body, LCY 948, and a Ghabbour-bodied Scania, LCY 965.

The present-day coach fleet includes a Volvo Première and Leyland Tiger, both of which have replaced their fire-damaged predecessors. The fleet is easily recognisable as individual artwork adorns the rear window of each coach, with colourful paintings of some of Malta's most attractive buildings.

Paramount Garages was founded by Joseph Grech. Originally the company was known as "The Assumption", a name which appeared on each of the vehicles. To begin with, during the 1930s, Joseph operated a bus, registration 3217, on the Cospicua to Valletta route. Then, in 1944, he purchased a permit for the Birkirkara route and converted a military truck into a bus. But then one of Joseph's relatives, on his return from New York, saw this newly painted bus (which was already sign-written with "The Assumption"!), told Joseph that "This bus is super. You should call it Paramount, because it is the best." The decision was made to adopt this name for the company. The sign-writer charged £2 to undertake the repainting, Joseph recalled.

Joseph was then requested to operate a school service for pupils who lived at Mgarr. Gradually the firm increased these schools services with Paramount maintaining many for British forces stationed on the island without tenders being invited, as the service provided was known for its reliability and punctuality. Each of the school services was allocated a route number, and this practice proved to be the forerunner of the system eventually adopted for the route buses on the island, when the colour-coding for the routes was abandoned and all the buses were painted green.

On his retirement, Joseph handed over the running of the firm to one of his two sons, Leo. Leo now oversees the operation of eight route buses, four of which are the quartet of Dennis Dart buses on the island, fourteen coaches, minibuses and chauffeur-driven cars.

Cancu Supreme Travel which was founded in 1945 by the Abela family is based in Zejtun. "Cancu" is the family nickname of the founder. The firm's original vehicle, a Ford V8 with a Barbara body, carried the registration number 1754. Another private bus, which had a Wayne chassis with Barbara bodywork, was numbered 2673. In 1984 Cancu entered the coaching field and transferred this registration to their first coach, an AEC Reliance with Aquilina body. The company owns the only Optare Excel low-floor route bus on the island. At the end of July 2001 Cancu received the first two of the new generation of vehicles, a Chinese-built King Long low-floor bus and a King Long coach.

The company now owns a fleet of fourteen luxury coaches, fourteen route buses, three vintage buses, minibuses and chauffeur-driven and private hire cars. There are seventy full-time employees and ten part-time drivers. In addition, Cancu has a subsidiary association of transport contractors, called Island Coach Services. Thus there are a further 27 coaches linked to the firm.

Zarb Coaches is based in San Gwann and was founded in 1950. The firm originally operated coaches with Maltese bodywork on Leyland or AEC chassis imported from Britain. When government regulations were eased, Zarb were quick to realise the opportunity of importing vehicles from Britain, and vehicle types such as AEC with Plaxton bodywork appeared on the island in Zarb colours. The company is primarily a coach firm, but a few route buses are operated too, including an 11-metre coach recently rebuilt as a 10-metre route bus.

Arthur and John's was founded about 35 years ago. Four coaches are owned, and the fleet livery has always been black and red. The four vehicles are owned and driven by the four members of the Galea family of Balzan.

Oxley Coaches is another family business, with just two coaches. The father of the present owner, Saviour Borg of Msida, founded the firm about 1950. Each season the two coaches are contracted to provide travel for holiday-makers with certain firms – in recent years with the Danish company "Dansk FolkeFerie", whose name appears on the coaches.

On 27th March 2002, two of Garden of Eden's vehicles were parked in Valletta's bus terminus proudly displaying their attractive artwork on their rear windows. LCY 921 depicts Mdina, the Silent City, and JCY 899 shows Mosta Dome.

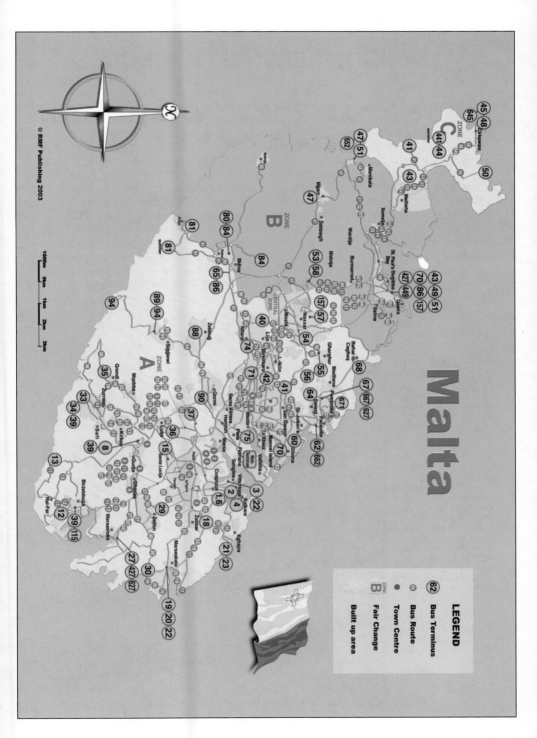

"MINIBUS SERVICE" MINIBUSES

This large fleet of minibuses operates tenders for tour operators, often as feeder services for holidaymakers between Luqa Airport and their hotels, or on contract services or on private hire duties. The fleet has a red and white livery. On the driver's door each vehicle carries the following details "PUBLIC TRANSPORT VEHICLE" in white capitals, "REG. No. GMY 109" appears below, and also "PASSENGER CAPACITY 17", or else other vehicles carry merely "MINI BUS SERVICE MAXIMUM NUMBER OF PASSENGERS 14". Some of the vehicles in the fleet now bear the operator's name and/or address. Until recently the fleet consisted entirely of Ford Transit vehicles, but the influx of other makes has added variety and interest, with some locally built Scarnif Sanfrans minibuses and most recently some Mudan minibuses from China. In addition, not all the minibuses remain painted red. A few have appeared in a darker, magenta, shade.

To save space in the list below all vehicles are listed by registration only. Every vehicle in the list is a Ford Transit M14 model apart from the following:

GMY 001	Toyota Coaster	M18		GMY 118	LDV Convoy	M17
LMY 006	Toyota Coaster	M18		HMY 150	Mudan	M18
GMY 009	LDV Convoy	M17		HMY 152	Scarnif Sanfrans	C18F
GMY 011	LDV Convoy	M17		HMY 164	Mitsubishi Rosa	M18
GMY 014	LDV Convoy	M17		HMY 166	LDV Convoy	M17
GMY 029	Scarnif Sanfrans	C18F		HMY 190	Isuzu	M17
GMY 031	Toyota Coaster	M18		HMY 239	Toyota Coaster	M18
GMY 043	Mudan	C18F		IMY 333	Toyota Coaster	M18
GMY 057	Mitsubishi Rosa	M18		IMY 351	Mudan	M18
GMY 066	LDV Convoy	M17		IMY 400	Scarnif Sanfrans	C18F
GMY 068	Scarnif Sanfrans	C18F (based on Gozo)		IMY 401	Scarnif Sanfrans	C18F
GMY 078	Toyota Coaster	M18		IMY 403	Scarnif Sanfrans	C18F
GMY 089	Toyota Coaster	M18		IMY 404	Scarnif Sanfrans	C18F

Three Ford Transit minibuses are parked in front of an imposing row of houses in Xlendi on Gozo on 12th April 2001. IMY 334 leads HMY 204 (since withdrawn) with IMY 307 bringing up the rear.

GMY 001	GMY 046	GMY 091	HMY 136	HMY 181	HMY 226	IMY 271	IMY 316	IMY 361
LMY 002	GMY 047	GMY 092	HMY 137	HMY 182	HMY 227	IMY 272	IMY 317	IMY 362
GMY 003	GMY 048	GMY 093	HMY 138	HMY 183	HMY 228	IMY 273	IMY 318	IMY 363
GMY 004	GMY 049	GMY 094	HMY 139	HMY 184	HMY 229	IMY 274	IMY 319	IMY 364
GMY 005	GMY 050	GMY 095	HMY 140	HMY 185	HMY 230	IMY 275	IMY 320	IMY 365
LMY 006	GMY 051	GMY 096	HMY 141	HMY 186	HMY 231	IMY 276	IMY 321	IMY 366
LMY 007	GMY 052	GMY 097	HMY 142	HMY 187	HMY 232	IMY 277	IMY 322	IMY 367
GMY 008	GMY 053	GMY 098	HMY 143	HMY 188	HMY 233	IMY 278	IMY 323	IMY 368
GMY 009	GMY 054	GMY 099	HMY 144	HMY 189	HMY 234	IMY 279	IMY 324	IMY 369
GMY 010	GMY 055	GMY 100	HMY 145	HMY 190	HMY 235	IMY 280	IMY 325	IMY 370
GMY 011	GMY 056	GMY 101	HMY 146	HMY 191	HMY 236	IMY 281	IMY 326	IMY 371
GMY 012	GMY 057	GMY 102	HMY 147	HMY 192	HMY 237	IMY 282	IMY 327	IMY 372
GMY 013	GMY 058	GMY 103	HMY 148	HMY 193	HMY 238	IMY 283	IMY 328	IMY 373
GMY 014	GMY 059	GMY 104	HMY 149	HMY 194	HMY 239	IMY 284	IMY 329	IMY 374
GMY 015	GMY 060	GMY 105	HMY 150	HMY 195	HMY 240	IMY 285	IMY 330	IMY 375
GMY 016	GMY 061	GMY 106	HMY 151	HMY 196	HMY 241	IMY 286	IMY 331	IMY 376
GMY 017	GMY 062	GMY 107	HMY 152	HMY 197	HMY 242	IMY 287	IMY 332	IMY 377
GMY 018	GMY 063	GMY 108	HMY 153	HMY 198	HMY 243	IMY 288	IMY 333	IMY 378
GMY 019	GMY 064	GMY 109	HMY 154	HMY 199	HMY 244	IMY 289	IMY 334	IMY 379
GMY 020	GMY 065	GMY 110	HMY 155	HMY 200	HMY 245	IMY 290	IMY 335	IMY 380
GMY 021	GMY 066	GMY 111	HMY 156	HMY 201	HMY 246	IMY 291	IMY 336	IMY 381
GMY 022	GMY 067	GMY 112	HMY 157	HMY 202	HMY 247	IMY 292	IMY 337	IMY 382
GMY 023	GMY 068	GMY 113	HMY 158	HMY 203	HMY 248	IMY 293	IMY 338	IMY 383
GMY 024	GMY 069	GMY 114	HMY 159	HMY 204	HMY 249	IMY 294	IMY 339	IMY 384
GMY 025	GMY 070	GMY 115	HMY 160	HMY 205	HMY 250	IMY 295	IMY 340	IMY 385
GMY 026	GMY 071	GMY 116	HMY 161	HMY 206	HMY 251	IMY 296	IMY 341	IMY 386
GMY 027	GMY 072	GMY 117	HMY 162	HMY 207	HMY 252	IMY 297	IMY 342	IMY 387
GMY 028	GMY 073	GMY 118	HMY 163	HMY 208	HMY 253	IMY 298	IMY 343	IMY 388
GMY 029	GMY 074	GMY 119	HMY 164	HMY 209	HMY 254	IMY 299	IMY 344	IMY 389
GMY 030	GMY 075	GMY 120	HMY 165	HMY 210	IMY 255	IMY 300	IMY 345	IMY 390
GMY 031	GMY 076	GMY 121	HMY 166	HMY 211	IMY 256	IMY 301	IMY 346	IMY 391
GMY 032	GMY 077	GMY 122	HMY 167	HMY 212	IMY 257	IMY 302	IMY 347	IMY 392
GMY 033	GMY 078	GMY 123	HMY 168	HMY 213	IMY 258	IMY 303	IMY 348	IMY 393
GMY 034	GMY 079	GMY 124	HMY 169	HMY 214	IMY 259	IMY 304	IMY 349	IMY 394
GMY 035	GMY 080	GMY 125	HMY 170	HMY 215	IMY 260	IMY 305	IMY 350	IMY 395
GMY 036	GMY 081	GMY 126	HMY 171	HMY 216	IMY 261	IMY 306	IMY 351	IMY 396
GMY 037	GMY 082	GMY 127	HMY 172	HMY 217	IMY 262	IMY 307	IMY 352	IMY 397
GMY 038	GMY 083	GMY 128	HMY 173	HMY 218	IMY 263	IMY 308	IMY 353	IMY 398
GMY 038	GMY 084	GMY 129	HMY 174	HMY 219	IMY 264	IMY 309	IMY 354	IMY 399
GMY 040	GMY 085	GMY 130	HMY 175	HMY 220	IMY 265	IMY 310	IMY 355	IMY 400
GMY 041	GMY 086	HMY 131	HMY 176	HMY 221	IMY 266	IMY 311	IMY 356	IMY 401
GMY 042	GMY 087	HMY 132	HMY 177	HMY 222	IMY 267	IMY 312	IMY 357	IMY 402
GMY 043	GMY 088	HMY 133	HMY 178	HMY 223	IMY 268	IMY 313	IMY 358	IMY 403
GMY 044	GMY 089	HMY 134	HMY 179	HMY 224	IMY 269	IMY 314	IMY 359	IMY 404
GMY 045	GMY 090	HMY 135	HMY 180	HMY 225	IMY 270	IMY 315	IMY 360	

GMY 068 is the sole Scarnif Sanfrans model to be seen on Gozo. It bides its time in Victoria Bus Station between tour duties on 4th August 2001.

FLORIANA AND PORTE DES BOMBES

In the following route descriptions reference is frequently made to Floriana and the Porte des Bombes, in particular, as all the routes leave Valletta this way.

Floriana is the suburb reached immediately after the roundabout at the junction with Triq Nelson. It takes its name from the engineer who designed the fortifications built as Valletta expanded during the seventeenth century. These fortifications were needed in the light of threats of invasions by the Ottoman Turks and were constructed during the fifteen years from 1635 to 1650. Along the main dual carriageway of St Anne Street are the US Embassy and British High Commission buildings. The Porte des Bombes stands at the western end of Floriana. It is an elegant Baroque gateway with three arched doorways which was constructed between 1697 and 1720 and formed part of the city's outer defences. Nowadays it is an imposing traffic island through which cars, but not buses, are allowed to pass.

On their way into Valletta, buses pass the Porte des Bombes and climb up towards St Anne Street, but then turn left on the approach to Floriana. For most of the day buses do not travel along St Anne Street. Instead they pass Argotto Botanical Gardens in Triq Sarria. After 18:00, however, buses are permitted to keep straight ahead along St Anne Street on their approach to the bus terminus.

Along Triq Sarria, on the right, is a huge open area, larger than a football field, called the Granaries. This is where the Knights of Malta stored a two-year supply of grain for the island in underground chambers, the stone lids of which are still clearly visible. Nowadays, the Granaries is an open area large enough to hold a crowd of up to 100,000, especially for political demonstrations and, in May 2001, for the visit of the Pope.

FBY 687 sets out for Santa Lucia on route 15 and is seen passing by the imposing buildings of Floriana, a minute or so after departing from Valletta Bus Terminus. *Paul Wigan*

ROUTES 1, 2, 3, 4 AND 6 TO THE THREE CITIES

Vittoriosa, Cospicua and Senglea are the three areas of the Cottonera district and they lie south of the Grand Harbour east of Valletta. They were granted the all-embracing name of the Three Cities by Napoleon's commander, General Vaubois, in 1798, in the vain hope that, by embellishing the residents' status, he would be able to win them over to accept new French legislation which was being introduced to the island.

The Three Cities had originally been settled by the Order of the Knights of St John after 1530; the Vittoriosa area of the Grand Harbour was known, in Italian, as il Borgo (the village), which the Maltese soon altered to a local variant "Birgu". Senglea was known as L'Isla, and Cospicua as Bormla. During the next century and a half, the Order regarded the creeks as strategically important in the defence of the island against Turkish aggression. The Margherita Lines and Cottonera Lines, which are a series of eight bastions around the landward perimeter of Senglea, Cospicua and Vittoriosa, were built.

During the Second World War, German and Italian aircraft bombed the dockyards situated on the creeks where these three towns lie. During April 1942, more than 3,100 tons of bombs fell on the Cottonera area; consequently little of historical value remains nowadays. The area was quickly rebuilt after the war, to enable the residents who had been evacuated to return home.

Buses serving the Three Cities pass through archways and tunnels to reach their destinations. Road signs on the approaches to the Three Cities bear the local names of the towns, too.

Senglea is named after the Grand Master Claude de la Sengle who allowed families to settle on the newly-fortified peninsula during the 1550s if they then built their new homes on the building plots which the Grand Master had allocated to them free of charge. The Turks mounted a huge attack on the peninsula about ten years later, in 1565. Over 8000 of them were killed but Fort St Michael was strong enough to withstand their attacks. Nowadays the area is famous for the Dockyards which can accommodate ships up to 300,000 tonnes. Bombed during World War Two, the peninsula has been rebuilt, as has the Church of Our Lady of Victory. This church was badly damaged in 1941 during an air-raid which was targeting the aircraft carrier HMS *Illustrious* in Dockyard creek undergoing repair.

FBY 655 is seen in Kalkara on route 4 on 29th March 2002. The ornate green balconies of the houses, which are a distinctive feature of Maltese architecture, are clearly in view, too.

EBY 518 emerges from the tunnel under St Paul's Bastion on its way to Vittoriosa on route 1 on Good Friday afternoon 2001.

In Vittoriosa the Inquisitor's Palace was originally the law courts and became the residence of the Inquisitor, the Pope's Apostolic representative, whose appointment on Malta was to oversee the enrolment of suitable Christians into the Order of St John. The Palace reflects the lives of these Inquisitors. The Collegiate Church of St Lawrence was where the lifting of the Great Siege of 1565 was celebrated; its relics include a silver processional cross from Rhodes which was used in the Crusades, and is always paraded during the City's *festa* on August 10th each year. Fort St Angelo is built on the original site of a Phoenician temple. During the Great Siege it was the focal point of the Turks' attacks. Later it became a prison, but its principal outline, following additional defences being built in the late seventeenth century, remains today. Under British rule the Fort was, successively, the HQ of the commandant of the barracks, a naval barracks, naval station and submarine base.

Kalkara lies outside the bastions which protect the Three Cities, on the peninsula between Kalkara Creek and Rinella Creek. It has a small harbour where traditional Maltese boats are repaired or moored during the winter. Fort Rinella, a nineteenth-century coastal battery, was built to accommodate a single 100-ton gun; the largest rifled muzzle-loading gun ever produced. Nearby are the Mediterranean Film Studios where naval or water-action scenes for international films are made.

Buses leave Valletta via Floriana, past the Porte des Bombes, and then travel along the dual carriageway through Blata l-Bajda and Marsa. After passing Marsa Shipbuilding, the buses reach Paola. Here all of the routes, except for route 3 to Senglea, continue ahead uphill along Triq Kordin skirting the northern limits of the island's prison. Triq Għajn Dwieli leads past Malta Drydocks and then to a tunnel under the fortifications of St Paul's Bastion which brings the Cottonera Marina into view.

Route 1
Valletta – Marsa – Paola Square – Ghajn Dwieli – San Gwann T'Ghuxa – Verdala – Vittoriosa Poste de Provence.

Departures from 06:15 to 21:45 from Valletta, Monday to Friday, every 30 minutes and from 07:20 until 22:10 from Valletta at weekends, with a journey time of 25 minutes.

Route 2
Valletta – Marsa – Paola – Ghajn Dwieli – San Gwann T. Ghuxa – Vittoriosa Town Square

Departures from 07:10 to 19:10 from Valletta, every hour, again with a journey time of 25 minutes.

Route 3
Valletta – Marsa – Paola Square – Fgura — Cospicua — Senglea

Departures from 06:00 to 22:00 from Valletta, and from 05:30 to 21:30 from Senglea, every 20 or 30 minutes, with a journey time of 20 minutes.

Route 4
Valletta – Marsa – Paola – Vittoriosa – Triq il-Missjoni – Bighi — Kalkara (circular route returning directly to Valletta).

Departures from 05:30 to 21:30 from Valletta, every 30 minutes, with the round trip taking one hour.

Route 6
Valletta – Marsa – Paola – Triq Ghajn Dwieli – Triq San Gwann T'Ghuxa – Cospicua.

Departures from Valletta from 05:30 until 22:00 roughly each hour, with a journey time of 25 minutes.

EBY 603 squeezes through the imposing gateway on the edge of Senglea town, having a minute or so before left the Senglea terminus, on 25th April 2000.

DBY 458 heads back to Valletta on route 6 on Good Friday afternoon 2001. The attractive balconies of the houses along Triq Ghajn Dwieli are to be seen, as are the fortifications of the Cottonera Lines in the middle distance.

Soon after the tunnel, the buses turn right up a short, steep hill. Whereas the summit marks the terminus of route 1, route 2 bears left into Vittoriosa and continues to the town's central square.

Route 3, however, follows its individual path by serving Paola more directly, passing the prison on the left, before turning left along Triq Bormla and then right at the next roundabout along Vjal it-28 ta'April, and then left into Triq Haz-Zabbar into Fgura. From here a left turn is taken at the roundabout at the junction of Triq Haz–Zabbar and Triq Hompesch, and then the bus heads down towards the fortifications, through Polverista Gate on the Cottonera Lines and passing the edge of Cospicua and onto the Senglea peninsula, where the terminus is the tree-lined town square.

On route 4, the bus continues past the terminus of route 1, along Triq San Dwardu and Triq Santa Liberata, and soon bears left by the Capuchin Convent onto the small peninsula. The bus then travels along roads at the back of Kalkara itself, so as to pass close to the entrance of the Rinella Film Studios, Rinella Battery and Rinella Creek. The bus swings left by the Trade School and descends to Kalkara Creek, travelling along the shore-edge past the grand St Joseph's Church. From here there is a short climb along Triq ix-Xatt tal-Kalkara to a picturesque arch back into Burgu and the terminus of route 1. Passengers travelling back to Valletta often have to change buses here.

ROUTE TO LUQA (AIRPORT)

Route 8
Valletta – Marsa – Paola — Tarxien – Bir id-deheb – Ghaxaq – Gudja — Luqa (Malta Airport) (circular).

For the first section of its journey to Luqa, this route covers the same roads as routes 1 to 6. From Valletta, the bus passes through Floriana, past the Porte des Bombes, and along the dual carriageway bearing downhill along Vjal it-3 Settembru to the complex junction near Marsa. Continuing straight on along Triq Aldo Moro (a four-lane stretch of road) the bus passes the premises of Marsa Shipbuilding. The shipyards and docks on the left are clearly visible with many tall cranes breaking the skyline view.

Marsa is the site of Malta's only racecourse, and this is where the island's trotting races are held which is one of the island's top spectator sports during the season which lasts from October to May. Arab horses compete in these races, and they are often to be seen on the public roads with their owners precariously perched on their trotting-carts hurtling along at break-neck speed.

The bus then bears right, along Triq Valletta on its approach to Paola, past the island's prison. Also built on the same area of land as the prison is a mosque. Turning right into Paola Square the bus passes the Church of Christ the King, a huge mock-Romanesque building of the 1920s.

Paola was founded in the seventeenth century as an overflow town for the population of the Three Cities. But, because it was built outside the fortifications, the town developed only slowly.

Paola is famous for the Hal Saflieni Hypogeum, an underground burial site, which is considered to be the island's finest archaeological monument. Discovered in 1902 during housing development, when builders who were cutting cisterns broke through its roof, the Hypogeum was the burial place for about 7,000 bodies, along with personal ornaments and pottery. The "Holy of Holies" chamber is believed to have been a burial place and a shrine. This temple complex is believed to have been in use for seven centuries from 3,700 BC until 3,000 BC.

MAN integral SÜ240 number AB23, formerly with **Deutsche Bundesbahn,** poses on the airport road system for a special photographic session for the author on 11th April 2001. Its Maltese registration plate is clearly visible, too.

DBY 465 approaches the main bus-stop at Luqa Airport on Easter Saturday 2000. The airport's well-tended lawns, and houses at Gudja in the distance are clearly visible.

The bus leaves Paola for Tarxien, eventually reaching the main road called Triq Tal Barrani, where it turns left and continues straight on until reaches the roundabout at Tal-imhammed near the premises of the Garden of Eden coach firm. Turning right for Ghaxaq, the bus wends its way through a one-way system, after which the bus bears left along the narrow roads through Gudja. The bus joins the main road skirting Luqa Airport, and threads its way through the Airport grounds to the terminus in front of the main Terminal Buildings. On the return journey through Gudja, the bus competes with oncoming traffic along some roads with "No Entry except for Route Buses" signs.

Tarxien is famous for its Neolithic Temples which date from about 3100 BC, and which were excavated between 1914 and 1919. In the South Temple the statue of a giant goddess is the most famous relic here – a large woman whose upper torso is missing, but whose full pleated skirt covers broad hips and legs. Tarxien is famed for its altars, sacrificial blocks, blocks decorated with animal friezes, stone bowls for burning aromatic herbs, beautifully paved courtyards and solidly carved wall slabs.

Gudja claims to be the birthplace of Gerolamo Cassar (1520 – 1586) who was the architect of many of Valletta's finest churches. In Main Street stands Palazzo d'Aurel, one of the island's finest country palaces, built during the eighteenth century. It is reputed that Napoleon Bonaparte and Horatio Nelson, accompanied by Sir William and Lady Hamilton were entertained here.

Departures from Valletta are every 20 or 30 minutes from 06:00 until 20:00, and from 05:30 until 20:00 from Luqa, with the round trip taking one hour. The 06:25 departure from Valletta on weekdays is numbered route 9 and serves the Drydocks.

ROUTES SERVING BIRZEBBUGA

Route 11
Valletta – Marsa – Paola Square – Tarxien – Bir id-Deheb – Birzebbuga — Pretty Bay

This route follows exactly the same roads to the roundabout near the Garden of Eden premises at Tal-imhammed near Bir id-Deheb as route 8 (q.v.). The bus then continues straight ahead past Ghar Dalam caves (q.v. route 127 to Marsaxlokk) to Birzebbuga.

Birzebbuga was once a fishing port, but the cranes and container-ships at the nearby Malta Freeport dominate the skyline nowadays. Buses turn left to follow the coast-road round to Pretty Bay. This bay boasts a broad expanse of cream-coloured sand alongside the bus terminus. The sand is always "topped up" by the local council after the winter. Palm trees line the roads in the town. Wharves and cranes of the Freeport dominate the whole beach area, and planes on approach to Luqa Airport fly low overhead.

Departures from Valletta begin at 06:00 and finish at 22:30; the first bus leaves Birzebbuga at 05:30 and the last at 21:00. Timings throughout the day are every 10 or 15 minutes. The fare is 15c. and the journey time is 30 minutes.

DBY 427 pauses in Triq il-Girgien in Tal-Papa estate soon after midday on 23rd March 2002

DBY 394 is seen at the Pretty Bay terminus of route 115 soon after 14:00 on 22nd August 2000. This vehicle is one of the few Mercedes Benz route buses on Malta and carries a distinctive body by Casha complete with a passenger door, which is an unusual feature on Maltese-built bodywork.

Route 12
Valletta – Marsa – Paola Square – Tarxien – Bir id-Deheb – St George's Bay – Pretty Bay — Birzebbuga —Tal Papa Housing Estate
Route 13
Valletta – *ditto to* Birzebbuga – Kalafrana – Hal Far (AFM HQ).

Route 12 operates as a duplicate service to route 11 as far as Birzebbuga, running at times which complement route 11. From the Pretty Bay terminus, the bus travels along Triq San Patrizu and turns right to serve the large residential area of Tal Papa. The bus makes a clockwise circuit of the estate. There are five departures from Valletta on Mondays to Saturdays, the first at 11:30 and the last at 19:30, though the Saturday timings vary slightly. There is just one departure on Sunday at 11:30.

Route 13 proceeds past the Freeport out into a stretch of countryside before arriving at Hal Far Industrial Estate which is built on the site of the World War Two RAF airfield. After travelling along Triq Ghar Hasan through the Estate, the bus reaches the outer terminus at Hal Far AFM Headquarters and returns to Birzebbuga.

This is primarily a workers' route with five early morning departures from Valletta between 06:00 and 19:30 and then one other at 18:10 on Mondays to Fridays, though timings and frequencies vary at weekends. The journey time is 40 minutes.

DBY 330 takes on more passengers in Santa Lucia on route 15 on 7th August 2001. This unique Ramco bus was rebuilt during 1999, with side windows from a Plaxton coach used for its front windscreen. The name "Ramco" for the bodywork is an anagram of the "Marco" who carried out the rebuilding. One of the ATP clocks and a typical bus-stop are clearly in view too.

Route 15
Valletta – Marsa – Paola Square – Santa Lucia (circular)

Again following route 8 (q.v.) as far as Paola Square, the bus then continues straight on up to the large roundabout on the outskirts of Tarxien. Immediately after the roundabout the bus turns sharp left into Santa Lucia, where the anti-clockwise loop through the village is regularly signposted by prominent arrowed "Bus Route" signs. The large and well-kept houses in this village were homes for members of the British forces during World War Two.

Departure times from Valletta are from 06:20 until 20:00, and from St Lucia from 06:00 until the last return journey at 19:15, with a round trip taking 40 minutes.

An interesting feature of route 15's daily timetable is that there no departures between 12:40 and 15:00. Instead route 115 operates, providing the alternative longer variation out to Pretty Bay.

Route 115
Valletta – Marsa – Paola – Tarxien – Santa Lucia – Tal-Barrani – Bir id-Deheb – St George's Bay – Pretty Bay

This route covers the same roads to Santa Lucia as route 15 and then travels along the main Triq Tal-Barrani to rejoin route 11 out to Birzebbuga and Pretty Bay. It operates seven times a day, during the early afternoon and late evening, instead of route 15. Departure times from Valletta are 13:10 (yet numbered route 15), 13:30, 14:00, 14:30, 20:30, 21:00 and 21:30, with a journey time of 35 minutes.

ROUTES TO MARSASCALA

Route 17
Valletta – Marsa – Paola Square – Fgura – Zabbar – Zonqor Point – Marsascala (circular)

This is an infrequent route which serves the roads on the northern side of Marsascala Bay. The route is very similar to that followed by route 19 (see below) from Valletta all the way to Zabbar and beyond. As route 19 it leaves Zabbar along Triq haz-Zabbar, but bears left into Triq iz-Zonqor. The bus travels clockwise around this headland, serving a swimming pool at Zonqor Point, before returning to Marsascala where route 19 is rejoined to make the circuit around the southern side of the Bay past the Jerma Palace Hotel and back to Marsascala terminus. The bus then returns directly to Valletta over the same route via Zonqor Point again.

There are six departures from Valletta on weekdays at 07:30, 08:30, 12:10, 15:10 17:30 and 20:10; and five at weekends at slightly different timings with the 12:10 departure omitted. The round trip takes eighty minutes.

Route 18
Valletta – Marsa – Paola Square – Fgura – Zabbar

This route follows route 3 (q.v.) as far as Fgura. Where route 3 turns left at the roundabout at the junction of Triq iz-Zabbar and Triq Hompesch, the Marsascala routes continue straight on along Triq Hompesch, up to the next roundabout where the Hompesch Arch stands on the outskirts of Zabbar. This arch was erected to commemorate the day when Grand Master Ferdinand von Hompesch consented to the proposal to elevate the village's status to a town. From here the road swings left into Triq Tal-labour, and then there is a right turn to bring the bus to Zabbar town centre.

EBY 493 operated the 15:10 departure of route 17 on 23rd March 2002 and is seen approaching Marsascala from Zonqor Point.

DBY 364 is seen on layover at the Marsascala terminus on Easter Sunday afternoon, 2000.

The splendidly ornate church, the Sanctuary of Our Lady of Graces, dominates the town centre. Its first stone was laid on 10th May 1641 and the church was completed 55 years later, with another fifty-nine years passing by before the gilding and ornamentation were finished. This church is a place of pilgrimage for those asking for intercession from Our Lady, especially if they are seeking help for children.

The town's great miracle has an even more recent history. On 14th October 1975, an RAF Vulcan bomber exploded over the centre of the town. All three of the plane's crew were killed, but only one resident died, struck by an electric cable severed in the blast. To this day the residents regard the event as a miracle.

Route 18 operates from Valletta from 06:00 until 22:00, and from Zabbar from 05:30 until 22:00. The timetable between 06:00 and 10:20 is unique, for it states "Rush hour" without qualifying the frequency of departures. Timings thereafter vary between every 10 or 20 minutes until evening, when departures are every thirty minutes. The journey time is 25 minutes and the fare costs 15c.

Route 19
Valletta – Marsa – Paola Square – Fgura – Zabbar – Marsascala (circular)

From Zabbar this route travels along Triq ħaz-Zabbar in rural surroundings to Marsascala which in recent years has been developed into a thriving, yet still simple, holiday resort. The bus route then makes a circuit of the town, travelling along the shoreline of Marsascala Bay, past the salt-pans to the four-star Jerma Palace Hotel and then back into town to the bus terminus overlooking the bay with its many cafes and restaurants alongside.

Just behind the Jerma Palace Hotel is Fort St Thomas, built in 1615, to prevent further invasions from the Turks attacking the Knights of St John. The more recent Zonqor Tower of 1886 vintage was built to provide covering artillery fire for the British.

Route 19 operates every 20 minutes from 06:30 until 21:00 from Valletta on weekdays, with four later journeys at 15 minute intervals until 22:00 at weekends. The journey time is 80 minutes for the complete return trip.

Route 20
Valletta – Marsa – Fgura – Zabbar Bypass – Marsascala

This route follows the same roads to the Hompesch Arch as routes 17 to 19. Whereas the other routes continue to Zabbar centre, route 20 turns first right after the Arch along Triq Sant'Antnin and passes the Park of Friendship on its approach to Marsascala.

This service operates hourly from Valletta from 08:50 until 19:50 on weekdays, and on the hour, from 08:00 until 20:00 at weekends, with a journey time of 35 minutes. The fare is 15c.

Route 21
Valletta — Marsa – Paola Square – Fgura – Zabbar – Xghajra

On reaching Zabbar this route heads along Triq ix-Xghajra and into Triq haz-Zabbar. Soon after the roundabout at Ta' Maggi, the bus turns left on its approach to Xghajra along the one-way Triq il-Knisja down to the coast to reach the terminus overlooking the sea.

This service operates every half-hour from Valletta on a circular service which takes 80 minutes, beginning at 08:20 until 20:20 . The weekend service is only hourly.

Route 22
Marsascala – Cospicua

This is a workers' service which has four early morning timings at 05:30, 06:15, 07:30 and 20:18. The journey time is thirty minutes.

EBY 554 swings sharply right away from the sea-front at Xghajra before attacking the steep incline up Triq il-Fortizza tal-Grazzia on 25th March 2002. A US Navy frigate can be seen in the background, as it makes its approach to Valletta harbour on a goodwill visit.

ROUTES SERVING ZEJTUN AND MARSAXLOKK

Route 27
Valletta – Marsa — Paola Square — Tarxien – Zejtun – Marsaxlokk (circular)

The first section of this route covers the same roads as route 8 (q.v.). Once past Tarxien the bus will regain the main road and after passing along Triq Tal-Barrani on the outskirts of Ghaxaq, the vehicle turns left to serve Zejtun.

Zejtun is an old agricultural village, known to have had its own parish as early as 1436. In May 1565 the first attacks of the Great Siege on the island took place here, when two young Knights were put to death by the invading Ottoman Turks, but not before they had given misinformation to their killers about the strength of the defending forces. Consequently the invaders made a number of strategic errors in their war plans. In 1614, well after the Great Siege, the Turks once again pillaged the town but were successfully and quickly forced back to their ships in Marsascala harbour by the Knights' cavalry. It was the last attack on the island by the Turks.

Lorenzo Gafa, the notable local Baroque architect, started the parish church of St Catherine in 1692. With its striking octagonal dome, the church is fine example of his work, with Doric and Ionic pilasters and two bell-towers adorned with Corinthian pilasters. The older parish church of San Girgor dates from 1436 and boasts the oldest dome on the island. The main door to the church is built off-centre, so that the Devil — who walks only in straight lines – will not be able to enter to disturb a church service. Within the church's thick walls, two narrow passages were discovered, in 1969, where the bones of more than eighty inhabitants of the village lay. The villagers are believed to have hidden there from Turkish invaders in 1547 and died in their hideout, when the church was set alight.

After serving the village centre, past the convent and church of San Girgor, the bus passes the ribbon development of houses and offices at Bir id-Deheb close to the Garden of Eden premises. At the nearby traffic-lights, the bus turns left, and soon passes the vineyards of Marsovin, the island's principal vine-growers. Soon Marsaxlokk is reached. Passengers alight at the sea-front, close to the open-air market stalls which sell fish, vegetables, fruit, local lace and tablecloths, souvenirs and handicrafts daily. Sundays are the best time to visit the markets here; extra bus services are provided on the routes to Marsaxlokk to cater for the influx of tourists. Recent pedestrianisation of the Town Square has meant changes in the terminus of the routes in the village. Buses now lay over in Triq L'Arznell which runs parallel to the main esplanade.

Marsaxlokk is a very pretty fishing village, where the traditional colourful *luzzu* fishing boats with a Phoenician Eye (a good luck charm) painted on the prow are always to be seen moored close by. Marsaxlokk was the site of the first attack by Mustapha Pasha's army of what was to become known as the Great Siege, on 19th May 1565. The 1614 invasion of the island was started here, too, but the Turkish invaders were frightened off by the guns of Fort St Lucian and landed at nearby Marsascala, then to attack Zejtun.

In 1798 Marsaxlokk was one of the five landing-places chosen by Napoleon Bonaparte in his attempts to capture the island from the Order of St John. His forces landed without resistance. Later Lord Nelson and his fleet took on supplies here whilst blockading the French forces in Valletta.

FBY 684 allows passengers to alight at the sea-front bus-stop in Marsaxlokk on 29th July 2001. The market stalls, palm-trees and blue decorations erected in time for celebrations to mark the Assumption are clearly in evidence, as is the bus's advertisement promoting the various day-tickets available to intending passengers.

Much more recently the harbour was the venue for the summit meeting between Mikhail Gorbachev and US President George Bush in 1989; a meeting which is now viewed as ending the Cold War. Locals still talk about the bad weather during the weekend of the summit, when the infamous winter *grigal*, a violent north-easterly wind, whipped up the waters in the harbour, where their naval ship was anchored.

Close to Marsaxlokk harbour stark examples of the island's recent industrialisation can be seen. A large electricity generating station near Delimara Point and new Freeport across Marsaxlokk Bay towards Birzebbuga are clearly visible.

The route operates every half an hour from 06:15 until 21:30 from Valletta. However, on Sundays, there is a more frequent timetable to enable passengers to visit the large market on the seafront, with departures from 06:30 until 21:30 — but services are every ten minutes or better between 10:00 and 16:00 during the winter timetable, whereas the summer timetable on Sundays varies between every ten and every fifteen minutes. The round trip on this route takes seventy minutes. Recent newspaper articles have intimated at the forthcoming improvements to the timings on this route. The fare is 15c.

EBY 484 pauses near the flats on the outskirts of Qajjenza on its approach to Marsaxlokk on 9th August 2001.

Route 127
Valletta – Marsaxlokk

This is a supplementary service which differs from route 27 only in its approach to Marsaxlokk. Instead of turning left at the traffic lights near to the Garden of Eden premises, the bus continues straight on towards Birzebbuga. It soon passes the Ghar Dalam cave complex, where remains of dwarf elephants and hippopotamus dating back 180,000 years, bones and antlers of deer, and human remains from the Neolithic and Bronze Ages have been found. Shortly before reaching the outskirts of Birzebbuga, the bus turns left through the residential area of Qajjenza before reaching more open land where the Enemalta LPG depot overlooking St George's Bay is situated. This coast-road bears left towards the southern end of Marsaxlokk Bay and the bus then threads its way round the back of the town to the terminus in Triq l'Arznell.

Route 28
Zejtun – Cospicua (Drydocks)

This is a mornings-only workers' route with three departures from Zejtun at 06:15, 07:45 and 08:20. The journey time is fifteen minutes.

Route 29
Valletta – Zejtun

This route terminates in Zejtun and covers exactly the same route as route 27 in so doing. It operates from Valletta from 06:00 until 22:00 and from Zejtun from 05:30 until 21:30 throughout the year. The fare is 15c.

FBY 736 arrives at the St Thomas Bay terminus of route 30 on 27th July 2001. Two of the attractively-painted *luzzu* **fishing boats are to be seen lying just off shore.**

Route 30
Valletta – Zejtun – St Thomas Bay (circular)

This route, too, covers the same roads to Zejtun, from where it passes through the village centre and to an extensive residential area of the town. Turning left onto the country road leading to St Thomas Bay, the bus soon arrives at its seaside terminus which is a picturesque spot with cream-coloured rocks on the beach.

There are only seven departures a day on this route and only four on Sundays. Buses leave Valletta at 07:15, and then at roughly two-hourly intervals from 08:15 until 18:20. After a very short stop at St Thomas Bay buses return to Valletta. The round trip takes one hour forty minutes.

Route 427
Bugibba/Qawra — Marsaxlokk

This is one of the island's "Direct" services linking the holiday resorts on the north coast directly with Marsaxlokk without going via Valletta. From Qawra Bus Station the route passes along the coast through Bugibba to St Paul's Bay, from where the main road to Mosta is followed (see Route 44). Continuing towards Valletta the route bypasses Lija and Balzan, then passes close to San Anton Gardens (see route 40). A fast stretch of road along the Mriehel By-pass soon brings the bus to Marsa with its Racecourse where route 27 is joined for the remainder of the journey to Marsaxlokk via Paola and Tarxien.

This route has only three timings from Qawra, at 09:15, 10:15 and 16:00, with a return journey from Marsaxlokk one hour later. As this is a Direct route, fares cost 40c whatever distance is travelled.

EBY 503 passes through St Andrews on its journey to Marsaxlokk on route 627 on Easter Sunday 2001.

Route 627
Bugibba/Qawra – Sliema – Three Cities – Marsaxlokk

This is the other "Direct" route between the same towns. However, on leaving the Bugibba and Qawra area, this service covers the main coast-road around the north of the island to Sliema via all the townships served by routes 60 to 68. After passing along Sliema Front the bus turns right, away from the coast, and climbs up to serve Gzira and the University along the dual carriageway to Marsa. On Wednesdays to Sundays only, the route threads its way through the Three Cities (q.v. routes 1 to 6) to serve the Rinella Movie Park near Kalkara where many sea or water-action scenes are shot for major films. It is quite usual in summer to see enemy submarines, sailing-ships, masts and icebergs floating here. From Rinella, the bus travels via Fgura to Tarxien where the usual roads to Marsaxlokk are followed.

On weekdays and Saturdays this route operates from Qawra at 09:30, then hourly from 11:00 until 15:00, with a return journey from Marsaxlokk at 10:45, then hourly from 12:15 until 16:15, via Tarxien and Paola Square to Sliema, omitting the Rinella Movie Park.

The Sunday timetable is more frequent – every 30 minutes – to provide easy travel for visitors to the Sunday market on the seafront at Marsaxlokk.

ROUTES TO ZURRIEQ, QRENDI AND HAGAR QIM

Route 32
Valletta – Marsa – Luqa – Zurrieq

After covering the main route to Marsa the bus makes almost a 360 degree circuit of the one-way system to be able to head out to Luqa, passing Malta's golf-course which adjoins Marsa Sports Club with its tennis, cricket and rugby football pitches. A left turn into Triq Valletta is followed by a long but gentle hill through the light industry units where the Scarnif busbodying factory is situated, and then Luqa village is reached. Originally an agricultural settlement established in 1634, Luqa nowadays gives its name to Malta's International Airport. The area suffered badly during the Second World War, being reduced to rubble by enemy aircraft. It is now rebuilt and proudly affluent.

The bus passes the headquarters of Air Malta, skirts the western edge of the Airport, passing through a tunnel beneath the runway, then turns right then left at two successive roundabouts and travels along the main Triq Valletta before turning left into Zurrieq town centre.

Zurrieq is the largest village in the south of Malta. Its church, dedicated to St Catherine of Alexandria, dates from 1632 and boasts six magnificent paintings by Mattia Preti, who designed the vault of St John's Co-Cathedral in Valletta. Around the town are three Roman towers and a number of smaller historic chapels.

This route operates from 06:20 until 18:.45 (and one other later departure at 22:00) from Valletta, with two journeys each hour. The journey time is half an hour and the fare 15c.

EBY 595 stands at Zurrieq terminus on Easter Saturday afternoon 2000, prior to working back to Valletta on route 34. The church of St Catherine of Alexandria overlooks the scene. Its two clocks (as on many Maltese and Gozitan churches) are there to confuse the Devil who roams. One clockface is real, the other trompe-l'oeil. Local superstition tells that, as the devil cannot tell the time, he therefore cannot come to collect departing souls.

Route 33
Valletta — Marsa – Luqa – Il-Karwija – Safi — Zurrieq

This operates only in the early morning, primarily as a workers' service. Its only difference from route 34 is that it omits serving Kirkop and instead runs parallel to the southern edge of the airport past barracks and the aircraft works at Il-Karwija before serving Safi.

Route 34
Valletta – Marsa – Luqa – Kirkop – Safi – Zurrieq

This route follows the same path as route 32 until the first roundabout after the runway tunnel. Carrying straight on at the roundabout the bus passes through the narrow streets of Kirkop and Safi, two delightful and affluent villages, before serving residential suburbs of Zurrieq.

The route operates every 30 or 40 minutes from Valletta, from 07:30 until 21:30, and from Zurrieq from 06:30 until 22:00. The journey time is 35 minutes and the fare is 15c.

Route 35
Valletta – Marsa – St Vincent de Paule Residential Home — Mqabba – Qrendi (circular)

After following the usual route to Marsa, this route serves the Marsa Industrial Estate by another road which runs parallel to the golf-course, before bearing left up to the main road with the St Vincent de Paule Residential Home at the junction. The bus turns left along the main road leading to Luqa Airport; it turns right under the runway tunnel, right at the next roundabout for Mqabba. It soon passes the large limestone quarries of Tad-Dawl. This limestone is used for building Malta's distinctive stone houses. Mqabba is soon reached and after negotiating two roundabouts the bus approaches Qrendi and turns right, up to the town square, which, as in so many other villages, is overlooked by a church, the Church of St Mary. The nearby Cavalier Tower, the only octagonal tower on the island, was built in the sixteenth century. In times of danger the local folk would take refuge in the tower and pour boiling pitch and throw stones from its flat roof onto the attacking forces.

The route operates from Valletta from 06:10 until 21:30, and from Qrendi from 05:30 until 20:30, every twenty or thirty minutes. The round trip lasts one hour ten minutes and the fare is 15c.

Route 36
Valletta — Luqa

This is a mornings-only daily workers' route with departures from Valletta at 07:00, 07:15, 07:30 and 09:00, with a journey time of 16 minutes.

Route 38 and its partner **Route 138**

Valletta – Marsa – Luqa – Zurrieq – Wied iz-Zurrieq — Blue Grotto – Hagar Qim – Qrendi – Valletta

Valletta – Marsa – Luqa — Qrendi – Hagar Qim – Wied iz-Zurrieq — Zurrieq — Valletta.

Route 38 follows the same path as route 35 to Qrendi and then heads out along narrow rural lanes towards the coast. Extensive views of the island's southern coastline come into view, with fields abundant with poppies in spring, farms, dry-stone walls and the bird sanctuary isle of Filfla out to sea.

Hagar Qim, and the nearby Mnajdra, are the sites of Malta's most important Neolithic temples, built about 3600 BC, i.e. one thousand years before Stonehenge. Hagar Qim stands on the cliffs which govern this stretch of coastline. It is a temple with several entrances and an intriguing external shrine. The largest stone weighs 20 tons and is over twenty feet in length. Many of the traditional "fat figures" of Maltese history (carved stone statues of grossly overweight deities), now in Valletta's museums, were discovered here. There are three temples at Mnajdra, tucked away in a hollow, and, as at Hagar Qim, they offer a wonderful view of the Mediterranean Sea.

The bus turns left at Hagar Qim and travels down the undulating and picturesque coast-road to Wied iz-Zurrieq, a pretty fjord in the precipitous cliffs from where a boat ride can be taken to the Blue Grotto and the caves formed under the cliffs. The bus now heads back inland to Zurrieq.

Route 38 operates at roughly hourly intervals from Valletta from 09:20 until 16:20. Route 138 operates from Valletta to Qrendi and then serves the Blue Grotto and Hagar Qim before arriving at Zurrieq. Departures from Valletta are from 09:45 until 16:45 at hourly intervals. Between them routes 38 and 138 provide a thirty minute frequency on the Hagar Qim and Blue Grotto section.

Route 39
Valletta – Marsa — Luqa Air Terminal – Zurrieq

This is an early morning workers' route.

FBY 669, a Bedford SB with Brincat bodywork arrives at Hagar Qim on route 138 on 27th March 2002.
Garry Luck

ROUTE 40 TO ATTARD

Route 40

Valletta – Msida – Birkirkara – Balzan – Lija – San Anton Gardens – Attard (circular)

From Valletta, the bus takes the main road to Msida and then serves Birkirkara. At the junction in Birkirkara where routes 43 et seq. turn right, route 40 continues straight ahead along Triq il-Wied. Birkirkara merges imperceptibly into Balzan hereabouts; the bus then turns right through the village, soon to return to the main road at the roundabout on the edge of Lija. Within the confines of this roundabout the route has its own bus-stop. A left turn and then a right turn take the bus through Lija, and at the junction with Triq il-Kbira, the bus turns right and passes through another part of Balzan.

A very sharp left turn into Triq San Antnin, a walled tree-lined road, brings the bus past the main entrance to San Anton Palace and Gardens. Route 40 is an intriguing route, for this section of the outward route involves the bus travelling against the traffic flow along otherwise one-way (almost single-carriageway width) thoroughfares.

Balzan, Lija and Attard are known as the "Three Villages" and boast of being "the places to live" on the island. They are quiet villages, with no industry, just a few shops but attractive houses and many *palazzi*, the patrician homes of the oldest Maltese families.

The main square in Balzan is dominated by the Parish Church of the Assumption which was erected in 1665 when the village became an independent parish. Lija is considered to be the most chic of the Three Villages and certainly has the greatest number of *palazzi*. Its Baroque parish church, the Church of the Saviour, was built in the late 1690s and has one of the earliest domes built on a Maltese church. Lija is noted for its *Festa* and fireworks display on 6th August – the largest on the island. In Attard, the Renaissance parish church of St Mary was designed by Tommaso Dingli in 1613; it was planned in the form of a Latin cross, has three domes painted in a deep pomegranate red and a pair of belfries. Its campanile was a 1718 addition. In Attard, too, there are numerous *palazzi*.

DBY 449 pauses in Balzan near to the Church of the Assumption, on Easter Saturday morning 2001.

FBY 774 reaches the end of the "one-way" system past San Anton Gardens. In this view, the bus is returning to Valletta from Attard, so it is, in fact, travelling the "right" way along the one-way system! The photograph was taken on Easter Saturday morning 2001.

The President of Malta is the most celebrated resident of the Three Villages, for, since 1974, his official residence has been San Anton Palace. The palace was originally built, in 1620, merely as a private country residence for the French knight Antoine de Paule who used it as his summer home. Once appointed as Grand Master he extended this residence into a palace, because he considered the journey from Valletta to Verdala Castle near Dingli (q.v. route 81) too irksome. Work began on these extensions in 1623 and the palace became the home of later Grand Masters, too.

The palace is not open to the public, although its terraces are. The gardens themselves are one of Malta's highlights. They are planted with trees, such as palms, pines and jacarandas and the paths are laid out in a formal grid pattern, with fountains and a pond at the intersections. The gardens have been open to the public since 1882.

If passengers alight from the bus on route 40 along Triq San Antnin for the gardens, they will find Villa Bologna behind the high walls on the opposite side of the road. A Maltese aristocrat, Nicola Perdicomati Bologna, built it in 1745 as a wedding gift for his daughter. It is one of the island's biggest villas, and is still in private ownership.

The bus continues along this "one-way" road, turns right into Triq il-Linja, a road which runs alongside the path of the former Malta Railway for almost its whole length. The bus now makes an anti-clockwise circuit of the residential area of Attard which includes a double run along Triq Santa Katrina.

The return journey to Valletta is undertaken immediately, this being a circular route. Much of the return journey is the same, though the bus makes a dog-leg along Triq il-Mosta in Attard, which also involves a short section of "against the flow" travel along a one-way residential street, and the bus then takes a different route through Balzan past the Church of the Assumption, thus omitting Lija.

The route operates from Valletta from 06:00 until 20:30, and from Attard from 05:30 until 21:00, with departures every 15, 20 or 30 minutes. The journey each way on the circular route is 35 minutes. The fare is 15c.

ROUTES SERVING SAN GWANN AND BIRKIRKARA

Route 41
Valletta – Msida – Malta University – Kappara – Ta'-Zwejt – San Gwann (Naxxar Road) – Imrabat – Valletta (circular route)

From Valletta the bus passes through Floriana, past the Porte des Bombes, swinging left down the loop and under the dual carriageway, eventually to arrive at Msida. At the complex roundabout, the bus turns right and ascends the short, sharp hill to the Regional Road. Passing Malta University on the left and the national swimming pool on the right, the bus turns off the Regional Road at the next roundabout and travels along Kappara Hill through San Gwann, then along Triq Birkirkara which leads into Triq Bella Vista. At the junction of the main road to Naxxar (see route 65, too), the bus turns left, very soon to turn left again into Triq San Gatt in Ta'-Zwejt which marks the outermost point of this circular route.

The return journey rejoins the main Naxxar road, sharing it with route 65, descending to, and passing under the Regional Road, continuing straight ahead along Triq Birkirkara with the Sacred Heart Convent on the right. The bus passes through the Savoy and Gzira area and turns right off Triq d'Argens, climbing up along Triq tas-Sliema, turning left into the Regional Road, and then descending to the complex junction at Msida, from where it takes the main road back to Valletta.

Departures from Valletta are from 08:00 until 18:50, and from Ta' Zwejt from 07:20 until 19:10, every 15, 20 or 30 minutes, with a journey time of 20 minutes. The fare is 15c.

Route 42
Valletta – Msida (Triq d'Argens) – Imrabat—Ta'Giorni – San Gwann (Zwejt) – San Gwann Industrial Estate – Birkirkara Parish Church

From Valletta, 42 follows route 41 to the complex roundabout at Msida, where the bus heads along Rue d'Argens (the road which many of routes 60 to 68 to Sliema cover), turning left into Triq tas-Sliema. At the next roundabout, the bus turns right on the Regional Road for a few hundred yards to the next junction, where the Regional Road passes over the Pont (bridge) Guze Ellul Mercer. Here the bus leaves the Regional Road, passes under the bridge and heads for the Ta'Giorni area. After travelling along Triq Ta'Giorni, Triq il-Qasab, Triq Ta'Sebbuqa, Triq Santwarju and Triq Mensija, the bus joins the main road through San Gwann which routes 41 and 65 share. It turns right along this road, eventually turning left to serve the San Gwann Industrial Estate. The bus then turns right onto the dual carriageway, id-Dawret ta'Birkirkara, which route 58 covers between L'Iklin and the University of Malta.

At the next roundabout, the bus turns left into Triq Tumas Fenech to reach the terminus close to the Community Centre and modern Parish Church in Birkirkara.

Thus route serves the very northern area of Birkirkara, away from the main roads through the town which the routes out to Mosta, St Paul's Bay and beyond cover.

Nowadays, Birkirkara has a population exceeding 23,000. Back in the eighteenth century, as the parish became wealthier through increasing support from benefactors, the church dedicated to Saint Helena celebrated its first *festa* in 1738. This building is

DBY 399 on lay-over at the Birkirkara terminus of route 71 on 29th July 1999.

considered to be the finest example of Maltese Baroque architecture with an ornate interior of frescoes, carvings and paintings. Another church in the town is dedicated to Santa Maria but it has fallen into disrepair and has been abandoned.

Departures from Valletta from 06:00 until 21:30, and from Birkirkara Church from 05:55 until 20:45, every half-hour with a journey time of 40 minutes. The fare is 15c.

Route 71
Valletta – Floriana – Hamrun – Santa Venera – Fleur de Lys – Birkirkara

This route reaches Birkirkara by an altogether different route and in so doing it serves the southern area of the town. The terminus is close to the site of the town's former railway station on the long-defunct Malta Railway.

From Valletta, the bus passes through Floriana and past the Porte des Bombes, along the dual carriageway to Hamrun. The long main street of Hamrun, Triq il-Kbira San Guzepp, is lined with shops, and Hamrun imperceptibly merges into Santa Venera, where the remains of the Wignacourt Aqueduct run parallel to the road for about half a mile. This aqueduct was built in the early seventeenth century as part of the waterway which brought channelled spring water from Girgenti on the coast into Valletta. At the roundabout marking the borders with the area called Fleur de Lys, the bus turns right – up to now the route has been identical to routes 80 and 81 to Rabat, Mdina and Dingli (q.v.). The bus continues along Triq Fleur de Lys for most of its length to the terminus near the Old Station.

This terminus is only a few hundred yards from the junction with main road through Birkirkara covered by the Mosta and St Paul's Bay routes.

Departures from Valletta are from 06:00 until 22:30, and from Birkirkara from 05:30 until 22:00, with a journey time of 20 minutes. The fare is 15c.

The vehicle schedules for the Attard and San Gwann area which applied on 24th March 2002 provided a very rare opportunity to photograph together five of the dozen or so normal control vehicles which remain on the island. The quintet were rostered that day for routes 40, 41 and 42, all of which depart from stands below the ramparts of St James' Bastion. From left to right are: DBY 313, EBY 570, DBY 399, EBY 526 and EBY 537. No surprisingly, all five drivers requested copies of this photograph.

Route 74
Valletta – Floriana –Hamrun – Santa Venera – Birkirkara– Balzan (Corinthia Palace)

From Valletta this route follows route 71 as far as Hamrun where a right turn by the police station is made towards St Luke's Hospital. A left turn brings the bus into Triq Kappilan Mifsud. The bus then negotiates the large roundabout at the junction with the Regional Road and continues straight ahead along Triq il-Ferrovija and Triq Salvu Psaila to the terminus of route 71 by the Old Station at Birkirkara. Here the bus bears right to join the main road through Birkirkara for a few hundred yards along Triq Fleur de Lys. By the post office, where the main routes out to St Paul's Bay and beyond turn right, route 74 continues straight ahead, soon to turn left into another section of road called Triq il-Ferrovija. At the junction with Vjal de Paule the bus reaches the terminus by the Corinthia Palace Hotel.

Departures from Valletta are at 30 minute intervals from 06:30 until 08:30 throughout the week, with two further timings at 17:00 and at 18:00 on weekdays. The journey time is 15 minutes.

The short-lived Malta Railway Company was a metre-gauge system which operated from Valletta to Notabile (Citta Vecchia) – the Old City, and former capital of the island – at the foot of the hill on which Rabat and the silent City of Mdina are situated. Opened in 1883, the railway line served Hamrun, Birkirkara and Attard. A tunnel under the hill was later dug, with a 1 in 4 gradient, serving as an extension of the line to the outer terminus called Museum, on the far side of the hill, on the road from Mdina to Mtarfa.

The railway eventually boasted nine steam locomotives and about three dozen rather quaint four-wheeled carriages. The system reached its peak during the 1920s, when one and a half million passengers were carried annually, however its financial success was eventually threatened by the growing importance of both trams and buses covering the same routes and the system eventually closed on 31st March 1931.

The Old Station at Birkirkara still remains, and the track of the railway and the sites of Notabile and Museum stations are marked on road-maps.

ROUTES TO BUGIBBA, QAWRA, MELLIEHA AND CIRKEWWA

The many routes which serve the north-western and northern resorts are obviously some of the longest services on the island, with route 48 to Cirkewwa being the longest of all (over twenty-five kilometres) and being timetabled to take seventy minutes from Valletta.

All the routes follow the same roads across the island from Valletta to the St Paul's Bay area. While the frequencies on these routes may not be quite as great as those allocated to the Sliema service, a seven-minute interval is the norm for much of the day.

From Valletta, all the buses pass through Floriana, past the Porte des Bombes, swinging left down the loop and under the dual carriageway, eventually to arrive at Msida. Here the buses carry straight on at the complex road system where the Sliema services turn right. After passing beneath the Regional Road, buses climb up Triq il-Wied ta'l-Imsida to Birkirkara, one of the larger villages on the island with a population of over 23,000 living in its narrow, crowded streets.

At the western edge of the town buses turn right, skirting Balzan and Lija, passing Mosta Technopark. Mosta is soon reached, but not before a lengthy one-way system is negotiated, bringing all the outward routes along Triq l'Indipendenza before turning right into Triq il-Kbira, (rough with potholes) where car-parking often causes hold-ups in its narrower sections. At the centre of the village, a sharp left turn brings the bus to the bus-stop for Mosta Dome.

The Mosta Dome is the usual name by which the parish church of the Assumption is known. Begun in 1833, when Mosta was still a small village, the Dome took 28 years to be built. The dome itself was constructed without the use of scaffolding because it was built over and around the original village church which had become too small for the growing parish and could not be demolished until the new church was finished. On completion the Dome was a source of controversy. The archbishop refused to bless the new church himself, as he did not approve of the circular plan of the church, preferring the traditional Latin form of the crucifix. At that time the Dome was claimed to be the third largest unsupported dome in Europe. Since the 1950s, however, the church at Xewkija on Gozo has taken over third place; (*see route 42/43 on Gozo.*)

The church has a bright interior with sixteen windows, a lantern light, and a floor with a geometrical pattern laid in two different marbles. During World War Two, on 9th April 1942, a Luftwaffe bomb crashed through the dome but did not explode. The 300 parishioners at Mass escaped safely. The defused bomb is now on display in the church.

After the bus-stop at the Dome, the long straight Triq il-Kunstizzioni climbs up towards the roundabout at the head of the Targa Gap. Straight on at the roundabout, the bus soon begins the descent, crossing the Victoria Lines and swinging right round the sharp hairpin bend halfway down.

On the distant coastline the hotel skyline of St Paul's Bay, Bugibba and Qawra can be seen. The bus now passes through low-lying arable fields to Bur Marrad. Nearby, on the hillside of Gebel Ghawzara, stands the church of San Pawl Milqi (St Paul Welcomed) where, tradition has it, Paul, Luke and other survivors of the shipwreck in AD60 were cared for by Malta's Roman governor, Publius, whom St Paul converted to Christianity. The present church was built in 1620. Archaeological discoveries have

FBY 777 begins the ascent of the hill towards the hairpin bend and the Victoria Lines and Mosta, with the hotels and coastline of the Bugibba area clearly visible in the distance, on 19th April 2000.

shown that farming was carried out as early as the second century BC in the immediate surrounding area.

The next roundabout is at the junction of the bypass around St Paul's Bay to the left, and, on the right, the main road coming in from the northern coast-road from Sliema. All the routes from Valletta have covered the same roads to this roundabout. An individual survey of each route now follows.

Route 43
Valletta – Msida – Birkirkara – Mosta – St Paul's Bay – Mistra – Mellieha

At the roundabout the bus continues straight ahead, along the main road through St Paul's Bay, which until the turn of the twentieth century was a peaceful fishing village. But as the Valletta businessmen became more affluent, they decided to purchase their "summer houses" in the area — "away from Sliema", they would say – and so the popularity of the village grew.

The narrow road through the centre of the village soon opens out onto the shoreline of Pwales Beach. Here the bus turns right, skirts the sea edge through Xemxija, then climbs a steep hill to Mistra village, a growing holiday centre, and then descends Mistra Hill before tackling the more fiercesome Selmun Hill with its double hairpin up to Mellieha Ridge where at the roundabout, the Mellieha Bypass starts.

Continuing straight ahead here, the bus passes through the outskirts of Mellieha, then fights its way through the village centre, down a steep hill always lined with parked vehicles, to the terminus near the police station. Mellieha stands on the ridge overlooking the northern coastline and Gozo beyond. Its lofty position, however, still made it a favourite target for corsairs, seventeenth century privateers in the southern Mediterranean, who could easily land at Ghadira Bay, then seize the local inhabitants and sell them as slaves. It was not until the security provided by British naval vessels patrolling offshore at the start of the nineteenth century that the town began to flourish. The parish church of the Nativity of Our Lady dominates the skyline when viewed from Ghadira Bay.

Route 44
Valletta – Msida – Birkirkara – Mosta – St Paul's Bay — Mistra – Mellieha (Ghadira Bay)

This route continues on past the terminus of route 43 in Mellieha and then negotiates another double hairpin bend on its descent, travelling between dry-stone walls and oleander bushes, towards the coast. Ghadira Bay, one of the best sandy beaches on the island is soon reached. The terminus is at the nature reserve situated halfway along the dual carriageway fronting the sea. This nature reserve is formed on the old saltpans of the area – which gave their name to Mellieha itself, as "melh" is the Maltese word for "salt". Ghadira Bay is the scene of many Roman wrecks; Napoleon chose the bay as one of his landing points, when he overran Malta in 1798 and drove out the Order of St John. The British forces built pillboxes and trenches around the bay during World War Two to protect the area against enemy landing-craft.

Departures from Valletta are from 07:00 until 19:50 during the winter timetable every 20 or 30 minutes. The summer schedules are worked in conjunction with route 50 providing three departures each hour until 21:00. The summer Sunday service is more frequent with a minimum of four departures each hour. The journey time is 65 minutes to the Ghadira terminus. Departures from Ghadira begin at 07:00, too.

Route 45
Valletta – Msida – Birkirkara – Mosta – St Paul's Bay – Mistra – Mellieha – Cirkewwa

Once at Ghadira Bay, route 45 tackles the final hill on the road to Cirkewwa, climbing up Marfa Ridge past the Mellieha Bay Hotel. The Red Tower stands on this ridge; a terracotta-coloured building built by the Grand Master Lascaris in 1649 to protect the northern part of the island and also to act as one of the warning towers across the island. From the ridge-top there is an immediate descent along Triq il-Marfa. Eucalyptus and mimosa trees line the first part of the descent before a bleak section of road distinguished by the premises of an oil and petrol tanker company brings the bus to the coast again. A left turn, with views across to Comino and Gozo, soon brings the bus to the Paradise Bay Hotel and to the terminus at Cirkewwa. This is the main ferry terminal for Gozo; extensive rebuilding is currently being undertaken to provide more berths for the Gozo ferries and improved passenger facilities.

Departures from Valletta are from 05:35 at half-hour intervals until 10:30. Then there is a twenty minute service until 15:30, when the half-hour service is resumed until 21:00. This is the longest route on the island which takes seventy minutes for the complete journey, one way.

Despite its Leyland badge, DBY 370 is a Bedford SB with Barbara bodywork and is seen at the terminus of route 44 at Ghadira Bay on Easter Sunday afternoon 2001.

Route 50
Valletta – Msida – Birkirkara – Mosta – St Paul's Bay — Mellieha – Armier Bay

This is an hourly summer-only service which provides easy access to beaches close to the Marfa Ridge. Once past Ghadira Bay and having climbed up to the top of Marfa Ridge, the bus turns right along a very rough road, passing the lane down to the Ramla Bay holiday complex, then turning left, making a long straight descent to Armier Bay with its café and sandy beach. Further on, but unserved by route 50 is Ahrax Point, the northerly tip of Malta.

Route 441
Ghadira Bay – Popeye Village.

This is a shuttle service, interworked with the main Valletta route, hourly during the main summer months, but only two-hourly at Easter, between 10:00 and 16:00. A distinctive timetable for the route is displayed at the PTA office at the Ghadira Bay terminus. From here the bus merely travels along the coast in the direction of Mellieha to the first roundabout, where it turns right on the Mellieha Bypass for a few hundred yards, before bearing right along a narrow lane to Sweethaven (or Popeye Village), past some horse-riding stables and over some "sleeping policemen". Popeye Village was created as the set for the 1980 film *Popeye* which starred Robin Williams.

Route 49
Valletta – Msida – Birkirkara – Mosta – St Paul's Bay – Bugibba – Qawra

Having reached the roundabout on the outskirts of St Paul's Bay, the bus continues straight on (as all the routes do) but only for a few hundred yards, before bearing right down a one-way street, Triq Toni Bajjada, to reach the waterfront near to Gillieru Pier. The bus turns right passing St Maximilian Kolbe Church, and travels along the esplanade, lined with palm trees, bearing right by the pier at Bognor Beach into Bugibba's Islet Promenade. This road is lined with shops, snackbars, souvenir stalls, a dodgem track, and sports facilities. Bay Square is alive with cafés and gift shops. Bearing right near the Oracle Casino, the bus soon reaches the terminus at Qawra. During 2001, a bus-lane along Islet Promenade was created for buses travelling from Qawra in the direction of St Paul's Bay, along the section of the promenade which is otherwise one-way for all traffic.

Bugibba is a popular holiday centre and boasts a large number of time-share apartments and 2-, 3- and 4-starred hotels. Qawra, too, is a popular resort with fine hotels, many overlooking Salina Bay to the east. Route 49 operates from 06:00 until 21:30 from Valletta, and from 05:30 until 21:00 from Qawra, with departures at 7, 10 or 15 minute intervals. On summer Sundays the service is more frequent. The journey time is forty-five minutes with a maximum fare of 18c.

Route 58
Valletta – Malta University – Mosta — Targa Gap – Valletta (circular) (Mondays to Fridays)

Valletta – Malta University – Mosta – Bugibba – Qawra (Saturdays, Sundays and Public Holidays)

This route takes an altogether different way from the others in this group, once it arrives at Msida. It climbs up to the Regional Road, (the main dual carriageway across the island taking through traffic away from Valletta). It then continues along the Birkirkara by-pass past the extensive grounds of Malta's University and then past Malta's largest hospital, with the narrow streets of Birkirkara on the left and the San Gwann Industrial estate on the right. At the roundabout at the junction with Triq in-Naxxar, the bus turns right, thus rejoining the main road and bus routes to Mosta

FBY 781 pauses at the bottom of the hill near to Mellieha (Ghadira Bay) on route 645 on 12th April 2001. This particular bus-stop marks the start of Zone 3 fares — which cost 20c from Valletta.

and beyond. Vehicles travelling inward to Valletta turn left by Lija cemetery along Triq San Mikiel and Triq Geronimo Abos through L'Iklin – especially on school-days.

During weekday mornings until 11:00, the terminus of route 58 is the roundabout at the top of Constitution Hill in Mosta, at the Targa Gap. After 11:00 the route continues through to Bugibba and Qawra. At weekends and on public holidays the 58 serves Qawra, throughout the day. The route from Mosta to Qawra is as route 49.

Route 58 operates from Valletta from 06:30 until 20:00 (irrespective of its Mosta or Qawra destination) every 20 or 30 minutes. Departures from Qawra or Mosta are 06:00 until 20:00. The journey time is thirty minutes to the Mosta terminus, or fifty minutes to Qawra. The fare is a maximum of 18c.

Route 48
Qawra – Bugibba – St Paul's Bay – Xemxija – Mistra – Mellieha – Marfa – Cirkewwa

This is one of the "Direct" routes on the island, providing an easy link with the Mellieha area and the Cirkewwa ferry terminal for the holidaymakers and residents of Qawra and Bugibba.

The route simply leaves Qawra along Islet Promenade, bearing left into Triq il-Halel, thus avoiding the bus-lane, and serves some of the hotels and apartment blocks away from the seafront in Bugibba. It soon arrives at the roundabout by the St Paul's Bay bypass, turns right onto the main route taken by all the routes to Mellieha, and thus covers the same roads thereafter all the way to Cirkewwa.

Route 48 operates from 08:30 until 18:15 from Qawra, and from 09:00 until 18:40 from Cirkewwa, in the summer (route 645 q.v. provides later timings). In the winter, the timings are: 08:30 until 17:00 from Qawra, and 09:10 until 17:40 from Cirkewwa.

Departures are every 15, 20 or 30 minutes with a journey time of half-an-hour. The fare is a standard 40c.

Route 149
Valletta – Msida – Birkirkara – Lija – Mosta – Burmarrad – Qawra

This hourly route provides yet another link between Valletta and the Bugibba area on weekdays from 06:10 until 19:20, with slightly fewer early morning timings from Valletta at weekends. Instead of serving the whole seafront at Bugibba, route 149 passes through the hotel area of Qawra prior to its arrival at the bus terminus. Otherwise its route is the same as the 49 throughout.

Route 645
Sliema Ferry – St Julians – Paceville – St George's – St Andrew's – Splash and Fun park – St Paul's Bay – Mistra Village – Mellieha – Cirkewwa

This is another "Direct " route which covers the main northern coastroad from Sliema (q.v. routes 60 to 68) past the outermost terminus of the Sliema routes (route 68) at Bahar ic-Caghaq and onwards to Salina on the outskirts of St Paul's Bay. Passing through Kennedy Grove, a popular grassy picnic area, the bus soon reaches the roundabout at the junction of the St Paul's Bay bypass. The bus turns right and continues to Cirkewwa, as if on route 45. Departures from Sliema are from 08:00 until 18.45, and from Cirkewwa from 09:10 until 20:10 during the summer. During the winter timings are 08:00 until 18:15, and 09:10 until 19:10, respectively. Departures after 08.45 are every 30 minutes, the journey time is 45 minutes and the fare is 40c.

ROUTES TO GOLDEN BAY

Route 47
Valletta – Msida – Birkirkara – Mosta – Skorba – Ta'Hagret Temples – Mgarr
Ghajn Tuffieha – Golden Bay

This route serves the rural and peaceful area north-west of Mosta towards the coast. From Valletta to the roundabout at the top of Constitution Hill in Mosta, the route follows exactly the same roads as the routes to Mellieha (q.v. routes 43, 44, 45). At this roundabout the bus turns left, past a VHF transmitter, to yet another roundabout, where it makes an almost 360 degree circuit before heading westwards towards Mgarr. Passing the southern extremities of the Victoria Lines at Falka Gap, the bus passes though Malta's least populated region, an agricultural area famed for its strawberries. On the approach to the small town of Mgarr, the bus passes the Skorba Temples, which are prehistoric sites dating from about 3600BC. These Temples and the Ggantija remains on Gozo (q.v. route 64 on Gozo) are credited as being the oldest free-standing structures in the world.

Mgarr is a quiet farming community which was first settled in the mid-nineteenth century. Its tall parish church has an incongruously small dome, which has been likened to an egg in an eggcup. The church was built by donations from the local parishioners, as so often on the islands. However, in this case, the poor farming community could afford to bring only produce from their farmholdings, which the parish priest then sold to raise cash.

Ta-Hagret Temples are close to the village square and also close by, is Mgarr Air Raid Dungeon which is reached through the Il-Barri Restaurant and which has been restored to provide a faithful evocation of how the Mgarr residents lived under shelter during the ferocious attacks on the island during 1941 and 1942.

EBY 512, on route 652, heads off along the Pwalles Valley towards Golden Bay in the early evening of 11th April 2001

DBY 313 is seen in Manikata, conversely, making a clockwise circuit through the village on Easter Saturday 2001.

In the Square the bus turns sharp right and proceeds uphill through the village along Triq Sir Harry Luke, named after a former Governor who wrote a detailed history of the islands. It turns left at the next T-junction, before descending through pleasant countryside past the Roman Baths which still show how sophisticated the Romans were, with changing rooms, lavatories, an early form of sauna, and heated pools.

The main road is lined with oleander bushes on the descent to the traffic island at the junction with the road from St Paul's Bay. Turning left, the bus approaches Ghajn Tuffieha Bay but then sweeps right, down the straight hill to Golden Bay. These two bays are separated by a gentle peninsula and are acknowledged as two of the island's best beaches. Nearby are a woodland tourist village and horse-riding centre.

Buses often complete their journey, on reaching Golden Bay. However, the village of Manikata on a nearby hillside overlooking the Pwalles Valley is served too, either by a double-run from this terminus, or, usually, by an anti-clockwise circuit begun by turning right at the traffic island mentioned in the previous paragraph, via Manikata and then to the Golden Bay terminus.

Route 47 operates from 06:10 until 17.37 from Valletta; from Golden Bay departures begin at 05:30 and end at 20:00, every thirty minutes. The journey time is 45 minutes. The fare is 18c.

Route 652
Sliema – St Julians – Paceville – St George's – St Andrews — Splash and Fun Park – Bahar ic-Caghaq – Bugibba/Qawra terminus – St Paul's Bay – Golden Bay

This is another of the "Direct" services on the island. As so many of the other Sliema-based routes, it follows the coast road through the holiday resorts and out to the Splash and Fun Park. The main coast-road eventually approaches Qawra and near to Kennedy Grove, the bus bears right up to the main road through Qawra overlooking

Salina. It soon arrives at the bus terminus at Qawra, from where it passes along Bugibba Islet Promenade before turning left away from the sea, to head to the roundabout at St Paul's Bay. Turning right here, the bus travels through the narrow streets of St Paul's Bay and at the roundabout at the head of Pwales Beach close to Xemxija, the bus heads off down the fertile Pwalles Valley where farming land and greenhouses are in abundance. The bus eventually joins route 47 at the traffic island near to Ghana Tuffieha where it, too, sweeps right, down to Golden Bay.

Route 652 operates from 08:30 to 18:00 from Sliema, and from 09:30 until 19:10 from Golden Bay, every 15 minutes during the summer. In winter, the timings are much the same but with a 30 minute frequency instead from 08:45 until 18:00 from Sliema, and from 09:30 until 19:00 from Golden Bay. The fare is 40c, irrespective of the distance travelled.

Route 51 is a short-working which covers the Bugibba/Qawra to Golden Bay section.

Route 46
Mgarr – Valletta
This is another workers' service, with three early morning departures from Mgarr at 06:30, 07:30 and 07:45.

Route 52
Valletta – Msida – Birkirkara – Mosta – St Paul's Bay – Manikata – Ghajn Tuffieha – Mgarr – Valletta
This route has three early morning timings from Valletta, at 06:00, 06:45 and 08:15. The route is merely a combination of the main route from Valletta to St Paul's Bay, from where the bus follows route 652 along the Pwalles Valley and then turns right to travel up to Manikata, before arriving at the Golden Bay terminus. Here the vehicle merely resumes its journey back to Valletta by covering route 47 via Mgarr.

This is, by far, the longest circular route on the island, lasting almost two hours.

DBY 381 is seen negotiating the narrow roads of Manikata at about 09.15 on 28th March 2002.

ROUTES TO NAXXAR AND GHARGHUR

Route 54
Valletta – Naxxar (school bus)
There are six morning departures on this route at 07:15, 07:35, 07:45, 07:52, 08:10 and 08:30. Each is scheduled to take 40 minutes.

Route 55
Valletta – Msida – Birkirkara – Naxxar – Gharghur

For much of its way from Valletta this route follows the same roads as routes 43 et seq., all the way to Birkirkara and past Lija cemetery. However, at the roundabout on the approach to Mosta Technopark, the bus turns right and begins the steady ascent of Triq tal-Labour which leads directly to Naxxar town centre where it circles the parish church and travels along Triq il-Parrocca to the roundabout. Here it turns left and almost immediately right, along Triq Gharghur. On the approach to Gharghur village, the bus bears right and then left into Vjal ir-Repubblika, continuing into Triq l'Oratorju where the terminus is in front of the church.

The return journey leaves along Triq in-Naxxar and thus serves the hamlet of Xwieki. The bus then turns right onto the main road into Naxxar, over the roundabout, past the church to the terminus at the top of Triq tal-Labour.

Route 55 operates from 06:00 until 21:40 from Valletta, and from 05:30 until 21:00 from Gharghur every 15 minutes, apart from a twenty-minute headway between 14:00 and 16:00, on weekdays. At weekends, the service operates every 20 minutes. The journey time is 35 minutes and the fare is 15c.

Route 56
Valletta – Msida – Birkirkara – Mosta – Naxxar – Gharghur

This route follows exactly the same roads to Mosta Dome as routes 43 et seq. Instead of turning left by the Dome, the bus continues straight ahead, past the Dome's main façade and heads out along the one-way Triq il-Kbira which leads directly into Vjal il-21 ta'Settembru. At the junction just past Naxxar Community Centre, the bus turns left into Naxxar town centre and follows the same roads to Gharghur as route 55. The return journey does not serve Xwieki, returning the same way via Triq Gharghur to Naxxar. On its approach to Mosta, the bus travels along Triq Sant Antnin, Triq Barrieri and Triq Oratorju throughout the one-way system.

Route 56 operates – mainly — every hour on the hour from Valletta from 06:00 until 19:00. The journey time is 25 minutes and the fare is 15c.

Naxxar stands to the northeast of Mosta on a hill which overlooks the surrounding countryside and the Victoria Lines. Naxxar church, dedicated to the Nativity of Our Lady, is a Baroque edifice. The Trade Fairground lies to the west of the town square where international and home-based fairs are regularly arranged. Nearby, the Palazzo Parisio is a finely decorated C19th "stately home", now much favoured as the venue for weddings and parties.

The Victoria Lines are a defensive barrier of fortifications about fifteen kilometres in length from Fomm ir-Rih Bay on the coast south of Mgarr to Fort Madliena on the northern coast close to the White Rocks Holiday Complex near Pembroke. These Lines were planned as an outer defensive barrier for Valletta. During the mid-nineteenth

DBY 356 climbs Triq tal-Labour on its approach to the town square in Naxxar on route 55 on 11th April 2001.

century the British army became increasingly worried about the development and increasing power of artillery fire. Thus attacks on the island would not necessarily involve an immediate assault on Valletta itself, rather an attack from further away. Army strategists proposed the idea of developing the natural feature of the Great Fault which cuts off the north of Malta from the rest of the island.

Thus the Victoria Lines, merely walls about six feet high, were built to provide cover for the army firing on attackers below. Work on building these defences was in progress from 1874 until 1897, being completed in Queen Victoria's Diamond Jubilee year – hence their name.

A subsidiary network of defences was also built on the ridge at Dwejra near Mosta.

Route 157
Valletta – Hamrun – Santa Venera – Birkirkara – Mosta – Santa Margherita and return (circular)

This is an hourly route from 07:10 until 19:10 on weekdays, and then only on Saturday mornings at the weekend from 08:10 until 13:10.

The route follows the same roads as route 71 all the way to Birkirkara, and then it covers the few hundred yards down to the main road through Birkirkara followed by the routes out to St Paul's Bay and beyond. In Mosta itself the route passes Mosta Dome and the premises of Paramount Garages on its way up Constitution Hill to the roundabout at the head of the Targa Gap, where it turns right along Triq id-Difiza Civili. After about half a mile the bus makes a full circuit of roads in the residential area of Santa Margherita, before returning directly to Valletta with a complete journey time of 70 minutes.

NAXXAR LOCAL ROUTES

Local government reorganisation took place on Malta in April 1994, and, amongst others, the new town council of Naxxar was created. One of its first projects was to establish a free circular daily bus service around the town which is wholly subsidised by the town council. This project remained unique on the island, no other town councils having followed the example set by Naxxar until 2003 when Sliema introduced a new town service.

The town route was introduced on 16th January 1995 with a civic ceremony marking the occasion. The first day's operations were provided by Bedford YLQ/Plaxton Y-0583 (now EBY 583), a vehicle owned and driven, appropriately, by a Naxxar resident, Mario Bonavia.

The service is provided Mondays to Saturdays throughout the year with one timetable in force during the school year and another during the summer holidays, thus catering for the local primary school's term-time and summer-school hours.

The bus departs from Naxxar bus terminus near the Church of Our Lady of Victory and turns almost immediately right into 21st September Avenue. Then the bus turns left into Triq il-Musbieh, and on along Triq il-Bjad, left into Triq il-Missjunarji and then right, along Triq l-Emigranti, where a fine prospect over Labour Avenue, the main road to Naxxar, and across to Mosta is to be had. The bus turns right into Triq l-Amerika and right again into Triq l-Ingilterra, then left into Triq il-Germanja, then right once again into Triq it-Tuffieh. The bus rejoins 21st September Avenue for a short distance before making an extremely sharp right turn into San Pawl tat-Targa along Triq Jean de la Vallette. The bus turns left into Triq Sir William Jervois, then right along Triq il-Freemental, crossing Triq ir-Raheb Kurradu, and along Jules Verne Street to the area of the town overlooking the Naxxar Gap. At the roundabout the bus turns right, along St Paul's Street heading back towards the town centre past the phone tower, joining route 55 to Gharghur. At the next roundabout the bus turns into St George's Street, turning left for the short stretch of Triq il-Haddieda, then right into Leli Falzon Street. Another very sharp right turn brings the bus into Guzeppi Stivala Street, then left down Mdina Road, and then right, up Labour Avenue (the main road into Naxxar), round the parish church and back to the bus terminus.

On 2nd August 2001, EBY 538 is about to depart from Triq San Gorg on the 12.15 timing of the Naxxar local service, which caters, primarily, for school-children returning home after their morning summer-school. The distinctive Town Council board is clearly visible in the windscreen of the bus.

The buses operating this service carry a distinctive board in their windscreens which bears the town's coat-of-arms of a red and white cross in a red and white shield and the legend Naxxar Local Council. Along the route there are distinctive bus stops also bearing the coat-of-arms and the inscription "SERVIZZ MADWAR IR-RAHAL. KUNSILL LOKALI NAXXAR".

Certain departures on this service operate to small townships nearby lying within the confines of Naxxar council, with route number 154. Certain timings each day serve Maghtab, the northern coast-road to the Coastline Hotel at Salina and Bahar ic-Caghaq. Route 154 is, therefore, unique amongst the bus routes on Malta, for it is the only numbered route not operated on behalf of the PTA, but for Naxxar Town Council.

On leaving Naxxar terminus, route 154 serves the southern part of the town, following exactly the same route as the Town service as far as the first roundabout at the Naxxar Gap. Here a panoramic view of Malta's northern coastline comes into view. After negotiating a difficult hairpin bend on the descent across the Victoria Lines, the bus reaches the tiny township of Maghtab, which is all too closely associated the island's gigantic landfill site. The bus soon reaches the main northern coast-road, turns left along it, and travels towards Qawra to the terminus at the entrance to the Coastline Hotel in Salina. The bus returns immediately to Naxxar by the same return route.

All the information relating to these routes is clearly posted at the bus terminus in Naxxar with the two timetables in force during the year clearly outlined in Maltese, only.

The "winter" timetable covers the period from late September until early July. Departures are timed at 07:15, 07:50, 08:45, 09:15, 11:40, 13:50, 14:30, 16:00, 17:00, 18:25 and 19:00, Mondays to Fridays. On Saturdays there is only a morning service, at 45-minute intervals from 08:30 until 11:30. The Monday to Friday timings at 08:45 and 11:40 serve Salina, Maghtab and Bahar ic-Caghaq. The 14:30 departure leaves from the primary school in Triq l-Iskola.

The "summer" timetable is less frequent, with departures at 08:00, 08:30, 09:15, 11:30, 12:15, 14:30, 17:00, 18:25 and 18:50, Mondays to Fridays. There are, however, four timings to Salina, Maghtab and Bahar ic-Caghaq, those at 08:30, 11:30, 14:30 and 18:50. The 12:15 timing departs from the primary school, when the summer-school finishes. The Saturday timetable offers just two journeys at 08:30 to Ghadira and at 12:00 from Ghadira back to Naxxar.

One of the distinctive Naxxar bus stops which bears the town's coat-of-arms of a red and white cross in a red and white shield and the legend Naxxar Local Council.

ROUTES TO THE SLIEMA AREA

Routes 60, 63 and 163
Valletta to Sliema (Savoy area)

All the routes from Valletta serving Sliema and its adjoining towns pass through Floriana and then past the Porte des Bombes. On the downhill run towards Pieta, buses pass by Ta' Braxxia Anglican Cemetery and then skirt the quays at Pieta and Msida along a tree-lined dual carriageway with a sweeping bend round to Msida. At the huge roundabout at Msida, buses turn right for Sliema.

From here the routes serve different roads to reach Sliema Front and beyond. Routes 60 and 63, as many others, pass along Triq d'Argens, but cover only the immediate neighbourhood of Savoy.

Route 60 continues along Triq Rodolfu, climbing past the Police Station up to Savoy, the old area of Sliema, away from the coast, on a slight hill. Vehicles reverse into the bus-bay at the terminus in Triq Nicolo Isouard. An interesting feature of the first section of the return journey is that the bus has to travel against the flow of one-way traffic along the narrow roads which distinguish this part of Savoy.

Route 60 operates from Valletta from 06.00 until 22.00, and from Savoy from 05.30 until 21.30. There are nine rush-hour departures from 06.00 until 09.00; thereafter the services operate hourly until 17.00, then half-hourly until 22.00. The journey time is a quarter of an hour; the fare is 15c, as it is on all routes in the area.

EBY 473 is the latest route bus on the island to have been extensively rebuilt. Caruana in Mellieha built its sleek new bodywork. It is seen opposite the Sliema Ferry terminal, operating route 66 on 28th March 2002.

Route 63 continues through Savoy past the terminus of route 60, descending Triq Adrian Dingli to the coast-road at St Julian's Point, where a right turn is made. The 63 now heads back towards Valletta and stays close to the coastline, passing through Tigne, once the site of a British army barracks and family quarters. This promontory is undergoing extensive redevelopment with residential blocks and shopping complexes being built. The remains of Fort Tigne face Fort St Elmo on Valletta's peninsula, both built to guard the entrance to Marsamxett harbour.

Route 63 operates every 30 minutes throughout the day on a circular route from Valletta from 06.45 until 20.20. The round trip takes 35 minutes.

Route 163

Valletta – Floriana – Pieta – Msida – Gzira – Savoy Terminus – Dingli Street – Sliema Seafront – Tower Road – Ferry – Ta'Xbiex – Msida – Msida – Floriana – Valletta (circular)

This circular covers the same roads as routes 60 and 63 and operates hourly from 09:30 until 12:30, then at 12:50, 13:10, 13:30, 15:30 and 16:30 on weekdays. At weekends it operates hourly from 09:30 until 12:30, and then hourly from 13:40 until 16:40. The round trip lasts forty-five minutes.

Routes 61 to 68 serve Sliema Front and beyond; the higher the route number (62 to 68) the further along the coast the outer terminus is. Between them the routes provide a very intensive service throughout the day, at five or ten minute intervals.

Route 61 to Sliema Ferry provides extra journeys on the main roads between Valletta and Sliema. There are four morning departures from Sliema at 09:00, 09:45, 10:07 and 10:30, but only two from Valletta at 09:40 and 10:25, A lonely lunchtime departure from Valletta is at 13:10, with no corresponding Sliema timing. Thereafter there are merely three late evening timings from Sliema at 09:30, 10:22 and 11:07, and from Valletta at 22:00 and 22.45. The journey time is thirty minutes.

Passengers board FBY 705 at the Savoy terminus of route 60 on 24th March 2002.

FBY 663 passes the Corinthia Hotel on route 66, on 28th March 2002.

Route 62 terminates at Paceville. Buses follow the main route outlined above to Msida, along Triq d'Argens, then bearing right along Triq Testaferrata, soon reaching the coastline and the main road, called "The Front" within Sliema, around the northern coast of the island. The broad road is Tower Road with, at its far end, the terminus for the Sliema Ferry across to Valletta. Here there are bus termini too, particularly for the express routes from Sliema.

The road follows the coastline indented with small coves, such as Balluta Bay and Spinola Bay, with a broad esplanade along the sea edge and many hotels overlooking the waters.

Sliema is the main residential area of the island as well as being the major holiday area. The town's early development took place as it was the resort favoured by the residents of Valletta and then became the place where the wealthier citizens of the capital wished to move to. Elegant villas in cream limestone were built and they brought a cachet to the area in the early twentieth century. Gradually the town's outer limits were extended as more and more residents wished to move to the area and Spinola and Balluta were developed. Hotels and apartments have replaced the elegant villas and dominate the waterfront nowadays.

At Balluta Bay there is a poolside lido where the Neptunes, one of the island's best water-polo teams plays its matches on Saturday evenings.

The road reaches its busiest junction at St Julian's, a bustling area full of restaurants, pizzerias and bars. At the top of Spinola Hill route 62 reaches its terminus at Paceville, by day an unprepossessing residential area, by night it is the island's most crowded and hectic venue for clubbers. Close by is the Portomaso development with a conference centre and the Malta Hilton Hotel, built around a man-made creek for yachts. Late-night buses serve Paceville to enable the clubbers to travel home to towns and villages all over the island in the early hours. These late-night routes are advertised on the side of some of the route buses.

Route 62 operates at ten or fifteen minute intervals throughout the day leaving Valletta between 05:30 and 22:50, with similar timings from Paceville terminus. The journey time is 25 minutes.

Route 64 continues on past Paceville to serve Swieqi, a well-heeled residential suburb. It terminates at St Andrews where the British garrison was stationed. Their barracks were built in the local limestone and, it is said, the plans of these barracks were intended for units in India but found their way to Malta instead. Nowadays they are used as private businesses or as government buildings. This circular route operates on the hour every hour from 06:00 until 20:00 from Valletta and the round trip takes eighty minutes.

Route 66 was introduced in June 2000 to cater for the extensive hotel developments around the Radisson Hotel in the Pembroke area. After passing through Paceville, the route turns right at traffic-lights onto Signal Road and, halfway up the hill to St Andrews, the bus turns right to make a lengthy circuit of the roads to the hotels overlooking St George's Bay, and it then returns to Valletta directly, without layover.

This circular route operates every 30 minutes from Valletta from 07:10 until 19:40 with the round trip taking forty-five minutes.

Route 67 continues up the hill from route 66's right turn to its terminus at St Andrews. The route has four early morning timings from Valletta between 05:30 and 06.23, and then returns as an evening service with nine departures between 20:45 and 22:00. The journey time is thirty minutes.

Route 68 travels further along the coast past holiday complexes and the Splash and Fun Park to its terminus on the main road at Bahar ic-Caghaq.

This route operates every 30 minutes from Valletta from 06:15 until 19:45, and two later timings at 20:20 and 21:20 at weekends. The journey time is thirty-five minutes.

Route 662
Valletta – Msida – Regional Road — Paceville, weekends only

This is an express service operating on Saturdays and Sundays on demand between 18:30 and 23:00 and takes twenty-five minutes.

Route 667
Valletta – Msida – Regional Road – St Julians – St Andrews.

This express route covers the usual route to Msida, where, at the large roundabout, it climbs the short hill to Regional Road, a fast dual carriageway which takes much of the direct traffic off the urban roads in the Valletta area, the Three Cities area and the Sliema area. This Regional Road eventually merges into the main road around the north of the island when it becomes Signal Road (see route 66). The St Andrews terminus is soon reached.

The route operates half-hourly from 06:35 until 09:35 and then hourly from 10:10 until 19:10 from Valletta, with a journey time of thirty minutes.

The latest import from Britain amongst the route buses is Dennis Falcon FBY 768, originally in the Hyndburn fleet. It awaits departure at Sliema Ferry on route 70 to Qawra on 27th March 2002.

Route 671
Valletta – Pembroke — St Andrews

This route serves all the usual places before reaching Pembroke where, on turning right off the main road just before the St Andrews terminus, it makes a circuit of the government housing developments close to the firing ranges of the Armed Forces of Malta. The route operates hourly from Valletta between 06:30 and 20:30 with a journey time of forty-five minutes.

Route 70
Qawra – Bugibba – St Andrews – St Julians – Sliema Ferry

This is another "Direct" route which links the two principal holiday areas on the island along the northern coast-road. The covered is much the same as route 652 (q.v.). It operates from 08:00 until 21:00 from Qawra and from 08:00 until 20:00 from Sliema at roughly 30 intervals, with a journey time of thirty-five minutes. The fare is 40c.

Sliema Local Route
On Monday 28 January 2003 Sliema Local Council introduced a new free bus service aimed at the local residents. This circular service (unnumbered) operates from Sliema Ferries at 08:00, 09:00, 10:00 and 15:00 and serves the town's residential area, with the aim of encouraging car-owners to leave their vehicles at home and to travel into town by bus. Following Naxxar's example, buses display a board in the windscreen bearing Sliema's red and white coat of arms and the inscription "SLIEMA LOCAL COUNCIL CIRCULAR TRANSPORT".

ROUTES TO MDINA, RABAT AND DINGLI

Route 80
Valletta – Hamrun – Santa Venera – Mriehel – Balzan – Attard – Mdina – Rabat

This route follows the same roads out of Valletta as route 71 (q.v.) as far as the roundabout at Fleur de Lys. Here route 80 continues straight on along a broad dual carriageway which borders the Mriehel Industrial Estate. At a busy T-junction the bus turns right onto the western extremity of the Mriehel Bypass which soon gives way to an attractive stretch of tree-lined road bordered by imposing and expensive houses on the edge of Attard. The centre of Attard is served by route 40 (q.v.).

The built-up area soon gives way to an avenue through fields divided by rubble walls. The bluff on which Mdina and Rabat are built is now in view, 185 metres above sea level. The imposing sight of Mdina's Baroque Cathedral stands out; in the valley to the right across the fields the floodlights of Malta's National Stadium can be seen, close to the Ta'Qali Crafts Village.

The bus begins the steep ascent of the hill to Mdina and Saqqajja Bus Terminus. However, on outward journeys the bus bears left at the summit (avoiding Saqqajja) to pass along a high-walled road by the convent on the approach to Rabat. The bus makes a full circle round the town, turning right into Triq had-Dingli, serving a suburb called Nigret, where a right turn is made at another roundabout, before reaching the bus terminus in Triq Santa Rita. On departing from here the bus bears right to pass by the Roman Villa on the edge of Mdina, before arriving at the bus terminus at Saqqajja.

Rabat and Mdina have been centres of population on Malta for centuries. The area is at the very heart of the region where Christianity was introduced to the island. In AD 60 St Paul is reputed to have slept for three months in a cave within a ditch beyond the walls of the old Roman town, after being shipwrecked on the coast. In the parish church of St Paul, first mentioned in documents as early as 1372, there is a huge painting of *The Shipwreck of St Paul* by Stefano Erardi. The Wignacourt College Museum displays the history of the College where the Knights who were hoping to become monks would reside. St Paul's Catacombs are an underground area containing numerous family burial plots of Punic, Roman, Jewish and Christian origins. These catacombs were cut out of live rock, and they form a labyrinth of tunnels and galleries. There is a chapel, and a main hall with agape (feasting) tables at both ends.

Timings on route 80 from Valletta begin at 06:25 and finish at 22:00; from Rabat at 05:30 until 22.00, with departures at 10, 15 or 20 minute intervals. The journey time is thirty minutes and the fare is a maximum of 18c.

Mdina is known as the "Silent City", and was the island's capital city until 1568, when the Knights of St John built the new city of Valletta, following the Great Siege. Since that time Mdina has boasted another name — Citta Vecchia (The Old City) — to distinguish it from Valletta. Mdina traces its history back to Phoenician times (800 to 480 BC), when the city covered an area three times the size it does nowadays. The town's name reflects the Arabic "medina", meaning "walled town", from the era when the Arabs took Malta, redrew the city's boundaries and rebuilt the fortifications which still exist to this day. Mdina has a tiny population. Its extremely narrow streets prevent much road traffic passing through. It remains one of the world's finest examples of a medieval walled city which is still inhabited. Some of Malta's patrician families still live here; the city's residents are the only people allowed to bring their cars in.

The vehicle which formerly carried registration FBY 646 was a Bedford SB with bodywork by Schembri of 1971 vintage. It operated route 81 on Easter Saturday 2001, and is seen pausing at the right-hand turn to the Cart Ruts, as some tourists alight to visit them. The trees mark the southern extremity of Buskett Gardens.

The Main Gate leads into St Publius Square, where the dungeons lie. The Palazzo Vilhena was the site of the mediaeval governing body of the island until the earthquake of 1693 devastated it. St Peter's Monastery, the Convent of the Sisters of St Benedict, is the home of about twenty nuns who are members of a strict enclosed order.

The floor plan of St Paul's Cathedral is laid out in the form of a Latin cross. The cathedral has a Baroque façade with two ornate belfries and an octagonal dome which dominates the skyline for miles around.

The Bishop's Palace has been the residence of the Archbishops of Malta since 1722. Its design incorporated smaller windows than those of the cathedral, as it stands on the town's fortifications.

Palazzo Falzon is the finest example of Norman architecture on the island and is now a privately owned museum which tells of the island's history over the past two centuries.

Bastion Square offers the finest views of the island. Originally an artillery position, this area has ramparts overlooking the terraced fields and the island's central agricultural plain, Mtarfa, the Ta' Qali Crafts Village, and in the middle distance Mosta Dome. Local inhabitants claim that smoke rising from Mount Etna on Sicily (over 60 kilometres distant) can be seen on a very clear day.

A very interesting variant of route 80 is now advertised (as from early 2002) on timetables at Valletta and Saqqajja termini, though information given remains confusing. There are two departures to Bahrija, twelve hours apart, at 05.15 and 17.15 on weekdays, and a third soon after 13.00 on Saturdays. These departure times refer to Saqqajja NOT Valletta, though this not clarified on the timetables.

Leaving Saqqajja, the bus skirts the walls of Mdina, passes the roman Villa and descends to the roundabout on the approach to Mtarfa. The bus now sets out along roads not otherwise covered by bus routes, past Ghajn Qajjet, to Fiddien Bridge through the Ghemieri Valley along Triq il-Kuncizzjoni. A left turn and a steady climb brings the bus to Bahrija village (shown as St Martin's on some local maps) some five kilometres west of Rabat. A further three kilometers distant is Fomm Ir-Rih Bay, a lonely but beautiful beach.

Route 81
Valletta – Hamrun – Santa Venera – Mriehel – Balzan — Attard – Mdina – Rabat – Dingli

This route covers exactly the same roads as route 80 to Rabat. After reaching the top of the Saqqajja Hill on the approach to Rabat, the bus follows the main road past the Roman walls. By St Dominic's Priory the bus bears left away from the urban area along fairly narrow and winding roads which lead to Verdala Palace and Buskett Gardens. At a crossroads close to the "Clapham Junction" cart ruts, a right turn is made and Dingli is soon reached. Passing close to the terminus, the bus makes a complete circuit of the village's residential area, during which the closest point of access by bus to Dingli Cliffs is to be found. The bus arrives back at the terminus where the driver often takes a short break before the return journey to Valletta.

Verdala Palace was designed in 1586 by Girolamo Cassar, the architect of St John's Co-Cathedral in Valletta, as a country villa and summer residence for the Grand Master Hugues Loubenx de Verdalle, a French cardinal. The palace looks very much like a traditional fortified mediaeval keep and today it is the official summer residence of the President of Malta.

The palace overlooks Buskett Gardens, which is Malta's most extensive wooded area. Originally the Gardens were developed as the hunting grounds for the palace where wild boar and deer were shot. The trees growing here include olives, oaks, pines and carobs; but few, if any, flowers grow here.

FBY 777 reaches the top of the ascent from Fiddien Bridge en route to Bahrija at about 17.45 on 27th March 2002.

The "Cart Ruts" are on a rocky plateau about 500 yards from the Gardens; they are 30 cm deep and 60cm wide and, although many instances are found in Europe, these Maltese "Ruts" are more numerous than anywhere else. Archaeologists still remain uncertain about their purpose and origin, but the Ruts are generally believed to date from Bronze Age (2,300 to 800 BC). A very recent proposition is that Malta is the surviving tip of Atlantis which was reduced to its present-day size by the earthquake which marked the end of the Neolithic period.

Dingli Cliffs are the highest in Malta, rising sheer form the sea to a height of about 750 feet.

Route 81 operates from Valletta from 05:50 until 21:30 mainly every 30 minutes during the day (09:00 until 18:30), whereafter it is hourly on a circular basis. Sunday services are slightly less frequent. The journey time is 50 minutes. Fares are a maximum of 18c.

Route 84
Valletta – Hamrun – Santa Venera – Mriehel – Balzan – Attard – Rabat – Mtarfa (circular)

This route serves Mtarfa, which is an expanding residential town outside Rabat. The town was formerly the site of British army barracks which were dominated by the David Bruce Military Hospital. The route covers the same ground as route 80, even as far as Nigret on the western edge of Rabat. Where the 80 turns right at the roundabout, 84 continues straight ahead, wends it way through a series of very narrow side-roads on the southern outskirts of Mtarfa, before making its way along the main road, past the school, and then turning right through a new housing development and circling its way back to the main road. Tracing its route back to the roundabout, the bus turns left and climbs back up the Saqqajja terminus at Mdina, as route 80 does too, passing on the way the Roman Villa and Greek Gate, which opens below Mdina into the wide ditch surrounding the City.

Departures from Valletta are from 07:20 until 19:10 at half-hourly intervals, generally. The round trip takes one hour forty minutes.

Route 65
Sliema Ferry – Sliema Front – Balluta – St Julians – Paceville – San Gwann – Naxxar centre – Mosta – Mosta Dome – Ta' Qali Crafts Village – Rabat

This is another of the "Direct" services across the island.

From Sliema the main route to Paceville is followed (q.v. route 62 et seq.). At the traffic lights on the junction with the Regional Road, the bus turns right onto the Road and passes under the tunnel at Ta'Giorni, and then takes the next exit for San Gwann. Travelling along the main road through the town, the bus is covering the same route here as route 41 (q.v.). After a stretch of dual carriageway the bus reaches a less built-up area, and passes the road on the left along which the premises of Zarb Coaches are located. Soon the outskirts of Naxxar are reached and for the next mile or so the main route into Mosta is followed which the Naxxar and Gharghur services also cover. In Mosta the bus travelling in this direction has to negotiate the lengthy one-way system along Triq il-Kungress Ewkaristiku and back along Vjal and Triq L-Indipendenza. The bus then turns left away from Mosta along Triq il-Kbira and a quick series of left and right turns on the approach to Ta'Qali soon brings the bus close to the National Stadium where the Malta football team play their home matches, for instance.

DBY 357 arrives at the bus-stop at Ta'Qali Crafts Village on route 65 from Rabat to Sliema, on 3rd August 2001.

The roads hereabouts are built along what was the runway for the former World War Two airfield. A mock Greek Theatre has been built here, along with an autocross track, aircraft museum and the extensive Crafts Village, where the island's famous glass factory is situated. At the next T-junction, the bus turns right, and in so doing, joins the routes from Valletta near to the start of the ascent of Saqqajja Hill up to Rabat and the Saqqajja Bus terminus.

Timings from Sliema begin at 08:30 and operate every half-hour until 17:30. Return journeys from Rabat are from 09:15 until 18:30. The journey time is 50 minutes, and the fare 40c.

Route 86
Bugibba/Qawra – Rabat – Mdina

This is another "Direct" service, for which the fare is 40c. The route needs only to be briefly outlined as it traces roads covered by many other routes.

From Qawra Bus terminus the bus follows the exact route of vehicles heading for Valletta, along Bugibba's Islet Promenade and then to St Paul's Bay, through Burmarrad, up the hill to Targa Gap, through Mosta along Constitution Hill to Mosta Dome. Here route 65 (above) is joined, and the bus similarly negotiates the one-way system and heads for Ta'Qali and Rabat along exactly the same route.

Timings are 09:00 until 17:15 from Qawra, and 09:30 until 18:00 from Rabat/Mdina, every 20 or 30 minutes.

ROUTES SERVING QORMI, ZEBBUG AND SIGGIEWI

Route 88
Valletta – Hamrun – Qormi/St Sebastian – Zebbug

On leaving Valletta and passing through Floriana, the bus continues straight ahead past the Porte des Bombes to Hamrun, a town large enough to boast two parishes, though with little to commend it to the tourist. The bus bears left by the convent along Triq hal-Qormi and then passes beneath the Regional Road at a large roundabout. Here it continues straight on, past a Maltapost parcels depot on the left, down a slight hill to another roundabout where the right exit is taken towards Qormi. The bus passes through the town which used to be called Casal Fornaro, as many bakeries used to be situated in the area. The Löwenbrau and Cocoa Cola factories and car showrooms are the businesses more obviously in evidence nowadays.

The route through Qormi takes the bus through the area called St Sebastian, along Triq San Bastjan and Triq il-Vittorja before short sections of other roads bring the bus circling onto the main "double-named" dual carriageway on the southern edge of the town. For a few hundred yards the bus has to head back towards Valletta before being able to cross over to the other carriageway. Interestingly the local road maps show that the individual carriageways have different names – Triq l-Imdina towards Valletta, Triq Guze Duca away from Valletta. The dual carriageway finishes near yet another roundabout. This area is Tal-Hlas which has a tiny church in fields to the right; the original building of 1500 was razed to the ground in the island's earthquake of 1693.

At this roundabout the bus continues straight on, soon turning right into Triq il-Helsien which leads directly to the terminus in Triq Sciortino in front of the library and post office.

Departures from Valletta are from 06:00 until 22:30, and from Zebbug from 05:30 until 22:15, every 10, 15 or 20 minutes. The journey time is 25 minutes and the fare is 15c.

EBY 598 negotiates Triq Santa Margarit on its approach to the Siggiewi terminus on 29th July 1999.

FBY 801 awaits its next return journey to Valletta at the Zebbug terminus of route 88 on 11th April 2001.

Route 89
Valletta – Floriana – Hamrun – Qormi — Siggiewi

For much of its way to Siggiewi, this service follows route 88. At the roundabout, where route 88 bears right for Qormi, the bus on route 89 continues straight ahead along the broad Triq Manwel Dimech. At the top of the slight incline the bus joins the "double named" dual carriageway at its eastern end, halfway along rejoining the path of route 88. Routes 88 and 89 divert again at the next roundabout and the 89 bus bears left along the main road to Siggiewi. The approach to the town centre involves negotiating the very narrow Triq Santa Margarit. The bus passes the parish church of St Nicholas, a magnificent example of Baroque architecture built between 1675 and 1693, and then it drops down a slight incline bearing right into the town square and the terminus by the police station. Siggiewi has a population of about 6,000 and lies in the heart of the island's southern agricultural region.

Route 89 operates from 06:00 until 21:30 from Valletta, and from 05:30 until 20:30 from Siggiewi, at 15, 20 or 30 minute intervals depending on the time of day. The journey time is 30 minutes and the fare is a maximum of 20c.

Route 94
Siggiewi – Ghar Lapsi

Another route in Siggiewi is really a seasonal extension of route 89, serving Ghar Lapsi. On Thursdays and Sundays during July and August some of the buses arrive at Siggiewi on route 89 and then continue to Ghar Lapsi, strictly speaking on route 94. Timings for this route are difficult to verify – there was certainly little information on display in Siggiewi in 2002 – but four departures were offered on Thursdays, at 08:00, 11:00, 15:00 and 20:00. On Sundays there were more, at 08:00 and 11:00, then hourly from 14:00 until 20:00.

The route takes the bus further on through the village, along Triq tal-Bir l-Kbir, left into Triq Lapsi and out into the rural area to the south. The bus serves the Tal-Providenza Residential Home for the handicapped, which is a religious-based charity-funded organisation. The bus now descends steeply to Ghar Lapsi, with a fine view of Filfla Island and the far less attractive reverse osmosis plant which provides the island with palatable drinking water obtained from the sea.

Ghar Lapsi, or Cave of the Ascension, attracts many local children to its small beach, along with scuba divers and local fishermen. The bus turns round in front of the café which is famous for its fish soup.

Route 87
Siggiewi – Dar Tal-Providenza

This is a morning timing at 07:30, for people working at the Residential Home.

Route 91
Valletta – Hamrun – Qormi/St Sebastian – Qormi (St George) (circular)

This route serves another area of Qormi and so its route from Valletta mirrors route 88 as far as Triq il-Vittorja in Qormi. The bus turns right off Triq il-Vittorja into Triq Anici, then left along Isqof Scicluna. A left turn brings the bus to the residential area of St George's, where it makes a clockwise circuit along Triq Rebbiegha and other narrower roads back to Pjazza Maempel. Here the bus turns left into Triq Oratorju, immediately turning into Triq Kardinal Xibberas, reaching the terminus at the end of the road. On the return journey the bus threads its way along Triq il-Kbira and Tri il-Ghaqda to rejoin the outward route near the Post Office, and so back to Valletta.

EBY 534 descends to Ghar Lapsi on route 94 (despite showing 89) on the 11:00 timing on 2nd August 2001. This former London Transport AEC is one of the very few route-bus Swifts on Malta still in its almost original styling.

ROUTE 75 TO GWARDAMANGA AND ST LUKE'S HOSPITAL

From Valletta Bus Terminus, this short route follows the main road through Floriana, past the Porte des Bombes out to Hamrun. It travels along the main road through Hamrun and then turns right by the main police station into Triq Ferrovija; keeping straight on, it passes through the township of Gwardamanga and reaches the terminus in front of St Luke's Hospital.

Route 75 operates from Valletta from 06:37 until 18:20 every 10, 15 or 20 minutes with a journey time of 20 minutes on weekdays. The Saturday service has a two-and-a half hour break between 12:30 and 15:00, and on Sundays the break is even longer – from 11:10 until 15:00.

An unusual feature of this route number is that many of the principal routes on the island include their own route 75 departure from their outer terminus at about 15.00 each day, so as to arrive at the hospital in time for the start of hospital visiting at 15.30. A rusting metal timetable giving details in Maltese of all these routes stands by the bus shelter at the Hospital terminus.

EBY 513 stands at the St Luke's Hospital terminus at about 17:25 on 23rd March 2002.

ROUTE 98 VALLETTA'S LOCAL ROUTE

This route is the only one to serve Valletta itself. The very nature of the capital city with narrow hilly streets and pedestrianisation of the principal shopping thoroughfares precludes the possibility of buses even entering the city's heart. So route 98 merely makes a full circuit of the main roads which surround the city along the harbours' perimeters. Valletta must therefore be able to claim to be the capital city with the fewest bus routes – one! — actually operating through its streets.

From the Bus Terminus, the bus passes in front of the Phoenicia Hotel and turns right downhill into Triq L-Assedju (Great Siege Road), passing the Government offices on the right. Overlooking Manoel Island and Sliema on the far shore, the bus passes the outer defence walls of the city with their bastions built at focal points to protect the city. At the eastern end of the Valletta peninsula the bus reaches Fort St Elmo, the site of the War Museum. Close by is the Mediterranean Conference Centre where the "Malta Experience", which is an audio-visual history of the city and island, is located. The bus now passes the Siege Bell which is rung at midday every day, and then it runs alongside the Grand Harbour where cruise liners are often moored. It then passes under Fort Lascaris by the Customs Offices, bearing right, away from the shoreline uphill to the outskirts of Floriana. The bus soon reaches the roundabout at the junction with Vjal Nelson which leads from the Bus Terminus, and then back to the terminus.

Departures are every half-hour from 06:30 until 09:00, thereafter hourly until 18:00 on weekdays. On Saturdays there are six timings, at 07:30 and hourly from 08:00 until midday. There are no services on Sundays. The circular trip takes approximately twenty minutes.

EBY 579 stops for two foreign tourists to climb aboard near the War Museum on route 98 on 24th August 2000.

NIGHT SERVICES AND CHRISTMAS ARRANGEMENTS

Paceville is one of the outer villages of the Sliema conurbation. Its bus terminus is the starting point for each of the Special Night Services which cater for the night-clubbers and disco-goers who have spent the evening and early hours in the cafes and clubs in the area. Seven routes cover many of the principal towns and villages on the island, apart from the western area beyond St Paul's Bay out to Mellieha. A standard fare of 50c is charged. Route 62 provides the most intensive service, operating every 30 minutes from 11.00 pm until 1.30 am every night, with further departures until 3.00 am during the busiest summer months. The corresponding return journeys from Valletta on route 62 operate every 30 minutes from 11.50 pm until 2.20 am. Route 49 operates at midnight and at 1.30am every night. The other routes are also timed at midnight and 1.30 am, but only on Fridays and Saturdays.

During the Christmas and New Year period, there are special services operating, too. On the night of Christmas Eve and on the night of New Year's Eve services from Paceville operate rather infrequently until 05:00 to most parts of the island. It is a Maltese tradition that many people celebrate away from home on these evenings, and the PTA caters for the revellers.

On Christmas Day itself a normal Sunday service is operated. Malta is one of the very few places in the Christian world where something approaching a normal daily bus timetable is operated. The services are well-advertised in advance; special provision is made for the bus drivers to have Christmas dinner at their homes with their families, as there is a two-and-a-half hour gap between service from 12:30 until 15:00. One of the first services to resume is route 75 to St Luke's Hospital for visiting time.

Extensive advertising of these routes is carried by some of the route buses.

ROUTE BUS INTERIORS

Many owners take great pride in their vehicles which are their "homes" for much of their working day. Many of the older vehicles on the islands – especially those with locally-built bodywork – proudly display a Madonna and Child in a glass case in the framework surrounding the driver's cab. Other vehicles have, instead, a Latin inscription painted on a decorative glass partition. Some buses may have both. In other vehicles a picture of the Madonna will be prominently displayed over the windscreen. Some drivers have photographs of their family or of their late parents, too. Over 98% of the inhabitants of the island are Roman Catholic, and the strong faith of the islanders is thus to be seen even on board the buses. This style of decoration is called *tberfil* and only a small number of skilled local artists tackle such complex work.

On Gozo, the interior of FBY 015 shows the Madonna and Child as well as its original, purely numeric, registration 3095. This is a rare, if not unique, instance on any bus on the islands.

BUS FARES AND BUS STOPS

Malta is divided into four travel zones for its fare-paying passengers. Zone A covers the eastern half of the island out as far as Mosta and Naxxar. The Central Zone is the conurbation of Mosta itself. Zone B lies west of Mosta and includes Dingli, Mgarr, Bugibba, Qawra and Mellieha. Zone C is the westernmost segment of the island near Mellieha.

The fares, shown below, are listed on prominent PTA signs around the island.

Passengers travelling One fare Stage	10c
Within the same Zone	15c
From Zone A to Central Zone Mosta or vice-versa	15c
From Zone B to Central Zone Mosta or vice versa	15c
From Central Zone Mosta up to Zone C or vice versa	15c
Between two Zones i.e. from Zone A to Zone Bor vice versa, from Zone B to Zone C or vice versa	18c
Between three Zones i.e. from Zone A up to Zone C and vice versa	20c
Special services	25c
Express services	40c
Children between the age of 3 and 10	10c
Senior Citizens (travelling all zones except one fare stage) using the "kartakzjan"	10c

Bus stops are primarily oval blue discs, with BUS STOP in white capital letters. Fare Stage signs have a red background with FARE STAGE in white capital letters.

In Mosta there are two stops which clarify the direction of travel of buses on route 47. Even so, unless passengers understand that "via Mgarr" refers ONLY to route 47, these details seem rather confusing! At some of the main termini on the island, bus stops identify the routes by name, as exemplified by this stop at Golden Bay.

ISBN 1 897990 97 9

© Published by *British Bus Publishing Ltd and Tom Johnson* , February 2003
British Bus Publishing Ltd, 16 St Margaret's Drive, Wellington, Telford, TF1 3PH
httm//www.britishbuspublishing.co.uk - Telephone: 01952 255669 - Facsimile: 01952 222397